# spiralize
## every day

**80 RECIPES TO HELP
REPLACE YOUR CARBS**

**DENISE SMART**

hamlyn

A Hachette UK Company
www.hachette.co.uk

First published in Great Britain in 2017 by Hamlyn,
a division of
Octopus Publishing Group Ltd.
Carmelite House
50 Victoria Embankment
London EC4Y 0DZ
www.octopusbooks.co.uk
www.octopusbooksusa.com

Copyright © Octopus Publishing Group 2017

Distributed in the US by Hachette Book Group
1290 Avenue of the Americas
4th and 5th Floors
New York, NY 10020

Distributed in Canada by Canadian Manda Group
664 Annette St., Toronto,
Ontario, Canada M6S 2C8

ISBN 978-0-600-63469-0

A CIP catalog record for this book is available from
the British Library.

Printed and bound in China

10 9 8 7 6 5 4 3 2 1

Standard level spoon measurements are used in
all recipes.

Eggs should be medium unless otherwise stated.

Always check the labels of readymade ingredients
to make sure they do not contain ingredients that
are not suitable if you are following a vegetarian,
vegan, gluten-free or low-carb diet. For vegetarian
recipes, check cheese labels to ensure they are
suitable for vegetarians.

# contents

# introduction

A spiralizer is an affordable, easy-to-use cutting machine with a selection of blades that you can use to create a variety of noodles and ribbons from vegetables and fruit. It's really quick and easy to prepare fruit and vegetables using a spiralizer, so it can help you save time. Spiralizing can also reduce cooking times because many of the vegetables and fruit prepared in this way can be eaten raw or just cooked very lightly, which also means that more nutrients are retained.

## spiralizing and a healthy diet

A spiralizer is the ideal gadget for health-conscious cooks because it can help you cut back on refined carbohydrates, such as pasta and rice, by replacing them with spiralized fruit and vegetables. This means you can enjoy your meals while eating fewer calories.

Carbohydrates make up an essential part of our diet and are needed for our main energy supply; they are available in three forms, sugar, starch, and dietary fiber. Some foods are high in carbohydrates, such as pasta, bread, and many processed foods, but by eating them in an unprocessed form, such as fruit and vegetables, you can absorb the best nutrients from them and

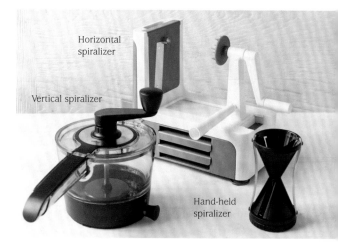

Horizontal spiralizer

Vertical spiralizer

Hand-held spiralizer

consume fewer calories. A three-ounce portion of cooked spaghetti contains about 270 calories and two ounces of carbohydrate compared to about 50 calories and half an ounce of carbohydrate for a bowl of spiralized zucchini made from 1 large zucchini.

A spiralizer will also encourage you to include more fruit and vegetables in your diet. It can be a life-saver for those following special diets, such as low carb, gluten free, paleo, and raw food. Always check the labels of preprepared ingredients if you are following a gluten-free diet to make sure they do not contain any wheat, either as an ingredient (for example, soy sauce) or through cross-contamination (for example, oats). Gluten-free versions are often available and can be used instead.

Cheese is a good source of protein if you are a vegetarian, but always check the label to ensure that it is suitable for vegetarians and doesn't contain animal rennet. Some hard cheeses, such as Parmesan, and other traditional cheeses, such as Gorgonzola and buffalo mozzarella, are still made with animal rennet, although increasingly cheese is being made with "microbial enzymes" or "vegetable rennet," both of which are suitable

---

**Each recipe in this book includes quick-reference symbols so that you can see at a glance whether a recipe is low carb, gluten free, vegetarian, or vegan.**

(gf) gluten free

(lc) low carb

(v) vegetarian

(vg) vegan

for vegetarians. Vegetarian pasta cheese is a great alternative to Parmesan cheese, and cheeses such as goat cheese, feta, ricotta, and mozzarella are also suitable.

## choosing a spiralizer

There are many brands on the market, but all essentially work in the same way. The larger horizontal and vertical type are better for heavier root vegetables and everyday use, but small hand-held spiralizers are ideal if you are cooking for one or for occasional use or for creating garnishes.

Spiralizers usually come with several different blades, each of which creates a different shape. For this book, I used a horizontal spiralizer with three blades, which I have called the ⅛-inch spaghetti blade, the ¼-inch flat noodle blade, and the ribbon blade.

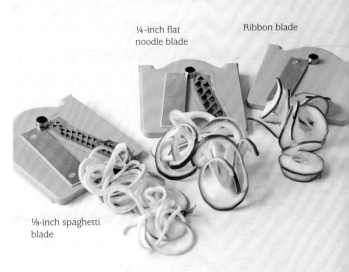

¼-inch flat noodle blade

Ribbon blade

⅛-inch spaghetti blade

### how to use a horizontal spiralizer

1 Attach the machine to the worktop using the suction feet or lever.

2 Insert the blade you wish to use into the machine.

3 Prepare the fruit or vegetable according to the recipe. Peel it, if required, trim off the ends to make a flat surface, and cut in half widthwise, if necessary.

4 Attach one end of the prepared fruit or vegetable to the blade and then clamp the other end of the vegetable to the spiked grip on the crank handle.

5 To create spirals or ribbons, grasp the side handle for leverage, turn the crank handle, and apply a little pressure to the fruit or vegetable so that it is

pressed between the blade and the handle.

6 Finally, remove the long core and a round disk that remains at the end of the spiralizing process (this can be chopped up and used to make soups, if you like).

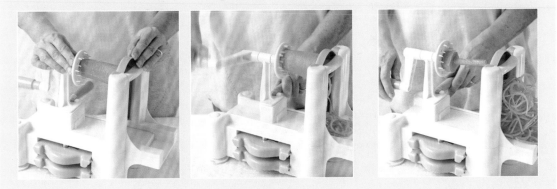

## how to make vegetable rices

1 Spiralize your chosen vegetable, using the spaghetti or noodle blade. Cauliflower should simply be broken into florets.

2 Place the spiralized vegetable or cauliflower florets in a food processor and pulse until the mixture resembles rice.

### tips for successful spiralizing

• Choose firm fruit and vegetables without pits, seeds, or hollow centers. The only exceptions are butternut squash (just use the non-bulbous end) and green papaya.

• Vegetables and fruit should not be soft or juicy. Pineapples, melons, and eggplants will fall apart when you spiralize them.

• Choose vegetables that are as straight as possible. Occasionally you may have to re-center the vegetables to avoid half-moon shapes.

• Make sure the ends of fruit and vegetables are as flat as possible by slicing a small piece off either end. Uneven ends can make it difficult to secure the fruit or vegetable to the spiralizer and may cause them to dislodge or misalign.

• If you find that a fruit or vegetable is not spiralizing very well, it may be because there is not a large enough surface area for the spiralizer to grip. For best results, lengths should be no longer than 5 inches and about 1 ½ inches in diameter. You can cut any large vegetables in half widthwise.

• You will be left with a long core and a round disk at the end of the spiralizing process. Save these cores to use when making soups or for snacks.

• A lot of juice is squeezed out of fruit and vegetables when you spiralize them, especially from zucchini, carrots, cucumber, potatoes, apples, and pears. Simply pat the spirals dry using paper towels before use.

• The blades of a spiralizer are very sharp, so use caution when cleaning your spiralizer. Wash the machine in hot, soapy water and use a small kitchen brush or toothbrush to clean the blades.

### cooking tips

• Spiralized vegetables can be eaten raw or cooked very quickly. The best cooking methods are stir-frying, steaming, or adding them to sauces and stocks. You can also bake and roast spiralized vegetables, such as potatoes, parsnips, beets, and butternut squash in half the time you would cook large chunks of the same vegetables.

• Some vegetable rices, such as beet, carrot, zucchini, and daikon radish, can be used raw. Alternatively, lightly sauté in a little oil or simmer in a little stock or sauce. They will need only a short time to cook.

• It is very easy to overcook vegetable spaghetti, so keep a close eye on it while cooking to make sure it doesn't fall apart.

• As a general rule, the harder the vegetable, the longer the cooking time.

• Make sauces thicker than you usually would since certain vegetable noodles, especially zucchini, will release extra juice into your sauce.

• Pat vegetables dry on paper towels, especially zucchini and cucumber.

• Cook your spaghetti or noodles separately, before stirring them into your sauce.

## storing tips

Most spiralized vegetables and vegetable rices can be stored in an airtight container in the refrigerator for up to four days. The exceptions are spiralized cucumber, which will only keep for about two days because of its high water content, and apples, pears, and potatoes, which quickly oxidize and turn brown and so are best prepared as needed.

## which fruit and vegetables can I use?

**Apples**  There's no need to peel or core apples. Simply trim the ends and spiralize them whole. The spiralized apple will turn brown very quickly so use immediately or dress with lemon juice.

**Beets**  There's no need to peel beets. Simply wash the skin, flatten the ends, and spiralize whole.

**Broccoli**  Broccoli stems spiralize really well, so when you cook broccoli don't discard the stems.

**Butternut squash**  To avoid the seeds, you should only use the non-bulbous end of the squash. Snip any really long strands of spiralized squash into smaller pieces using scissors.

**Carrots**  Choose large carrots for spiralizing.

**Celery root**  The best way to prepare this root vegetable is to use a sharp knife to remove the small knobs, peel the celery root, cut it in half widthwise, and trim it to make the ends flat.

**Cucumbers**  Once you've spiralized the cucumber you just need to pat the spirals or ribbons dry.

**Daikon radish (mooli)**  Spiralized daikon radish makes a great alternative to rice noodles.

**Green papaya**  You can find green papaya in Asian supermarkets. It can be attached to the spiralizer easily, even though it is hollow.

**Green plantains**  Choose plantains that are as straight as possible, and remove the tough outer green skin before spiralizing.

**Jerusalem artichokes**  Choose large artichokes. There's no need to peel these, so all you need to do is wash them. If you're not using the spiralized artichokes immediately, place them in a bowl of water with a little lemon juice to prevent them from discoloring.

**Kohlrabi**  Choose small kohlrabi about the size of a large apple. Prepare by peeling the outside and trimming the ends.

**Onions**  Onions can be spiralized whole. All you need to do is trim the ends before you start. You can use spiralized onions to replace chopped ones in recipes.

**Parsnips**  Choose large, fat parsnips for the best results when spiralizing.

**Pears**  Choose firm pears for spiralizing because pears that are too ripe will add too much moisture to some of the dessert recipes. Just trim down the pointed ends to prepare them for spiralizing.

**Potatoes and sweet potatoes**  Prepare potatoes by either scrubbing or peeling and then trim the ends and cut in half widthwise if very large.

**Turnips**  Peel off the outside skin and cut the turnip into large chunks with flat ends to attach to the spiralizer.

**Zucchini**  Forget about pasta! Spiralized zucchini makes a perfect spaghetti substitute.

# breakfasts and brunch

# apple and blueberry buckwheat pancakes with maple syrup

**Serves 4**

**Prepare in 10 minutes**

**Cook in 12 to 15 minutes**

2 red eating apples, ends trimmed

1 ¼ cups buckwheat flour

½ teaspoon salt

2 teaspoons gluten-free baking powder

2 tablespoons superfine sugar

1 ¼ cups buttermilk

1 egg

1 cup fresh blueberries

1 tablespoon sunflower oil

**To serve**

handful of blueberries

maple syrup or honey

Using a spiralizer fitted with an ⅛-inch spaghetti blade, spiralize the apple.

Sift the flour, salt, and baking powder into a large bowl and stir in the sugar. Beat together the buttermilk and egg in a pitcher. Gradually beat the buttermilk mixture into the flour to make a smooth batter. Stir in the spiralized apple and the blueberries.

Heat a large nonstick skillet over medium heat. Dip a crumpled-up piece of paper towel into the oil and carefully use this to grease the hot skillet. Drop 4 large, separate tablespoons of the batter into the skillet (to make 4 small pancakes) and cook for 2 to 3 minutes until bubbles start to appear on the surface and the underside is golden brown. Flip the pancakes over and cook for a further 2 minutes. Keep the pancakes warm while you cook the remaining batter, greasing the skillet with a little more oil if necessary.

Place 3 pancakes on each plate, add some blueberries, drizzle with maple syrup or honey, and serve immediately.

*Make these tasty breakfast bars in advance so you always have an energy-boosting snack on hand.*

# carrot and banana breakfast bars

**Makes 16**
**Prepare in 10 minutes**
**Cook in 35 minutes**

3 tablespoons coconut or olive oil, plus extra for greasing

3 tablespoons date nectar or honey

¼ cup crunchy peanut butter

2 carrots, about ½ lb, peeled, ends trimmed, and halved widthwise

3 overripe bananas

1 ¼ packed cups raisins or golden raisins

2 cups gluten-free rolled oats

Grease an 11 x 7 inch baking pan with a little oil.

Place the date nectar or honey, peanut butter, and oil in a small saucepan and cook over low heat, stirring from time to time, until melted.

Meanwhile, using a spiralizer fitted with an ⅛-inch spaghetti blade, spiralize the carrots. Coarsely snip any really long spirals in half using scissors.

Place the bananas in a large bowl and mash them with a fork, then stir in the spiralized carrots, raisins or golden raisins, and oats. Stir in the peanut butter mixture and mix well until all the ingredients are combined.

Spoon the mixture into the prepared pan and flatten the top with the back of a spoon. Bake in a preheated oven at 350°F for 30 minutes, until golden brown. Remove from the oven and let cool in the pan for 10 to 15 minutes. Mark into 16 bars and let cool completely in the pan. The breakfast bars can be stored for up to 2 days in an airtight container.

*These crunchy bars require very little cooking. All you need to do is toast the oats and quinoa.*

# peanut butter, quinoa, and apple bars

**Makes 8**

**Prepare in 5 minutes, plus chilling**

**Cook in 10 minutes**

1 ¼ cups gluten-free rolled oats

¾ cup uncooked quinoa

1 tablespoon chia seeds or flaxseeds

2 red eating apples, ends trimmed

½ cup crunchy peanut butter

½ teaspoon sea salt

3 ½ tablespoons honey

2 tablespoons apple juice

1 tablespoon coconut oil

Line an 8-inch square baking pan with nonstick parchment paper.

Spread out the oats and quinoa on a large nonstick baking pan and bake in a preheated oven at 350°F for 10 minutes, stirring once, until lightly toasted. Pour into a bowl and stir in the seeds.

Meanwhile, using a spiralizer fitted with a ¼-inch flat noodle blade, spiralize the apples.

Place the peanut butter, sea salt, honey, apple juice, and coconut oil in a saucepan and cook over low heat, stirring until the mixture is smooth and creamy. Stir in the spiralized apples and let cool for a few minutes.

Stir the peanut mixture into the oat mixture and mix until well combined. Spoon the mixture into the prepared pan and spread it out evenly. Chill in the refrigerator for about 1 hour or until the mixture has hardened and set.

Remove from the pan and cut into 8 bars. The bars can be stored for up to 3 to 4 days in an airtight container in the refrigerator.

*This buttery French toast is topped with caramelized pears.*
*If you prefer, you could replace the pears with apples.*

# cinnamon and pear brioche French toast

Using a spiralizer fitted with a ribbon blade, spiralize the pear.

Melt the butter and sugar in a large skillet, add the spiralized pear, and cook over medium heat for 5 to 6 minutes, stirring occasionally, until lightly caramelized. Set aside.

In a shallow dish, beat together the egg, cinnamon, and sugar and then beat in the milk. Add the slices of bread, let soak in the mixture for a few minutes, then turn them over and let stand until all the egg mixture has been absorbed.

Melt a little butter in a skillet over medium heat. Add the bread and cook for 2 to 3 minutes on each side, until golden. Serve immediately, topped with the caramelized pear.

**Serves 2**
**Prepare in 5 minutes**
**Cook in 10 to 15 minutes**

1 large pear, pointed end trimmed
1 tablespoon butter, plus extra for frying
2 teaspoons soft brown sugar

**For the toast**
1 large egg
½ teaspoon ground cinnamon
1 tablespoon superfine sugar
3 tablespoons milk
2 thick slices brioche bread

*This classic breakfast cereal is also delicious as a crunchy snack. It can be stored for up to 2 days in an airtight container.*

# honey-roasted apple granola

**Serves 4**

**Prepare in 10 minutes, plus cooling**

**Cook in 35 to 40 minutes**

⅓ cup honey

2 tablespoons coconut or olive oil

2 red eating apples, ends trimmed

¾ cup gluten-free rolled oats

¾ cup uncooked white quinoa

1 cup whole skin-on almonds, coarsely chopped

⅓ cup sunflower seeds

⅓ cup sesame seeds

**To serve**

milk or yogurt

fresh fruit

Warm the honey and oil in a small saucepan over low heat.

Meanwhile, using a spiralizer fitted with a ribbon blade, spiralize the apples.

Place the oats, quinoa, almonds, and seeds in a large bowl. Add the spiralized apples and mix well. Stir in the warm honey mixture to combine.

Spread out the mixture on a large nonstick baking pan and bake in a preheated oven at 300°F for 30 to 35 minutes, until golden, stirring once. Remove from the oven and let cool and harden.

Serve with milk or yogurt and fresh fruit.

*Combine the ingredients the night before and you will have a delicious breakfast ready in the morning.*

# fall fruits bircher muesli with almond milk

**Serves 2**

**Prepare in 5 minutes, plus soaking**

1 small red eating apple, ends trimmed

1 small ripe pear, pointed end trimmed

⅓ cup gluten-free rolled oats

1⅔ cups unsweetened almond milk, plus extra to taste

¼ cup chopped almonds

1 cup fresh blackberries

**To serve**

mixed seeds

maple syrup or honey

Using a spiralizer fitted with an ⅛-inch spaghetti blade, spiralize the apple and pear.

Place all the remaining ingredients in a large bowl, add the spiralized fruit, and stir to combine. Cover and let soak in the refrigerator for 2 to 3 hours, or overnight, to allow the oats to absorb the liquid.

Stir before serving and add a little extra milk, if a runnier consistency is preferred. Serve sprinkled with seeds and drizzled with maple syrup or honey.

*There is no need to precook the sweet potato because the steam in the waffle machine will cook it through.*

# sweet potato waffles with fresh fruit

Using a spiralizer fitted with an ⅛-inch spaghetti blade, spiralize the sweet potato.

In a large bowl, beat together the egg, buttermilk, melted butter or oil, flour, cinnamon, and baking powder. Stir in the spiralized sweet potato.

Preheat a waffle machine following the manufacturer's directions and spray with oil or brush with a little butter. Divide the batter between the 2 waffle plates, being careful not to overfill them, then cook for 5 to 6 minutes, until golden and cooked through.

Serve immediately with fresh fruit and drizzled with maple syrup or honey.

**Makes 2**
**Prepare in 5 minutes**
**Cook in 5 to 6 minutes**

1 sweet potato, about ½ lb, peeled, ends trimmed, and halved widthwise

1 large egg, lightly beaten

½ cup buttermilk

1 tablespoon melted butter or coconut oil

2 tablespoons buckwheat flour

1 teaspoon ground cinnamon

½ teaspoon gluten-free baking powder

cooking spray oil or melted butter, for cooking

**To serve**

fresh fruit, such as blueberries or raspberries

maple syrup or honey

*Perfect for brunch, these potato scones are so simple to make and are excellent topped with scrambled eggs.*

# easy skillet-fried potato scones

**Serves 2**
**Prepare in 5 minutes**
**Cook in 6 to 8 minutes**

1 russet potato, about ½ lb, peeled and ends trimmed

½ cup all-purpose flour, plus extra for dusting

¼ teaspoon baking powder

2 tablespoons butter, melted, plus extra for greasing

salt and freshly ground black pepper

Using a spiralizer fitted with an ⅛-inch spaghetti blade, spiralize the potato. Place the spiralized potato in a food processor and pulse until it resembles rice.

Place the flour, baking powder, and salt and pepper in a bowl, add the potato rice and butter, and combine gently with a spoon or your hands to make a dough.

Gently shape the dough into 2 balls using lightly floured hands, then transfer to a lightly floured surface. Roll out each ball into a circle about ¼ inch in thickness and prick it all over with a fork.

Heat a skillet over medium heat. When hot, carefully smear with a little butter, add the potato scones, and cook for 3 to 4 minutes on each side or until golden brown.

Serve immediately with the topping of your choice.

*These deliciously moist muffins can be served warm or cold. They will keep for up to 3 to 4 days in an airtight container.*

# pumpkin and oat breakfast muffins

Line a muffin pan with 10 paper muffin cups.

Using a spiralizer fitted with an ⅛-inch spaghetti blade, spiralize the pumpkin or squash. Coarsely snip any long spirals into shorter pieces with scissors.

In a large bowl, sift together the flour and baking powder. Stir in the oats and spices and mix well. In a separate bowl, beat together the eggs, buttermilk, maple syrup or honey, and the oil. Add the wet mixture to the dry ingredients and stir until just combined, then stir in the spiralized pumpkin or squash.

Divide the batter among the muffin cups, then scatter the tops with the pumpkin seeds. Bake in a preheated oven at 375°F for 20 to 25 minutes, until risen and firm.

**Makes 10**
**Prepare in 10 minutes**
**Cook in 20 to 25 minutes**

large chunk of peeled pumpkin or butternut squash (the non-bulbous end), about 10½ oz

1 ½ cups wholemeal flour

1 tablespoon baking powder

¾ cup rolled oats

½ teaspoon ground ginger

½ teaspoon ground cinnamon

2 eggs

¾ cup buttermilk

¼ cup maple syrup or honey

3 tablespoons coconut or sunflower oil

2 tablespoons pumpkin seeds

*If you prefer, you can top these corn and zucchini cakes with some crispy bacon.*

# corn and zucchini cakes

**Serves 2**
**Prepare in 5 minutes**
**Cook in 6 to 10 minutes**

1 corn on the cob

1 zucchini, ends trimmed and
    halved widthwise

4 scallions, thinly sliced

3 tablespoons self-rising flour sifted
    with ½ teaspoon baking powder

2 eggs, beaten

1 tablespoon sunflower oil, for
    frying

salt and freshly ground black
    pepper

**For the smashed avocado**

1 large ripe avocado

juice of ½ lime

2 tablespoons chopped fresh
    cilantro

½ red chile, seeded and finely
    chopped

Hold the corn cob upright on a cutting board and, using a large sharp knife, carefully slice off the kernels. Heat a griddle or nonstick skillet over high heat. Add the corn and cook for 2 to 3 minutes until blackened slightly, then transfer to a large bowl.

Using a spiralizer fitted with an ⅛-inch spaghetti blade, spiralize the zucchini. Coarsely snip any really long spirals in half with scissors.

Add the spiralized zucchini to the corn with the scallions, flour, and eggs. Season with salt and plenty of pepper, then mix well.

Heat a little oil in a large nonstick skillet over medium heat. Add 4 large, separate spoonfuls of the batter (to make 4 cakes). Fry them for 2 to 3 minutes on each side, until lightly browned and cooked through.

Meanwhile, halve, seed, peel, and coarsely chop the avocado. Place in a bowl with the lime juice, cilantro, and chile and smash together with a fork to combine coarsely. Season to taste.

Place 2 cakes on each plate and serve immediately, topped with the smashed avocado.

*Instead of potatoes, you can use a selection of vegetables, such as parsnips or turnips.*

# baked sausages and eggs

**Serves 2**
**Prepare in 5 minutes**
**Cook in 25 minutes**

2 large potatoes, skins scrubbed, ends trimmed, and halved widthwise

1 tablespoon olive oil, divided

4 pork sausages

6 mini portabellini mushrooms

2 slices smoked Canadian bacon

2 tomatoes, halved

2 large eggs

salt and freshly ground black pepper

tomato or steak sauce, to serve

Using a spiralizer fitted with a ¼-inch flat noodle blade, spiralize the potatoes.

Place the spiralized potatoes in a large bowl, add 2 teaspoons of the oil, season with salt and pepper, and toss well to coat in the oil and seasoning. Spread out the potatoes in a large, shallow nonstick roasting pan.

Bake in a preheated oven at 400°F for 5 minutes, then add the sausages and mushrooms. Drizzle the mushrooms with the remaining oil. Return to the oven and bake for a further 10 minutes, turning the sausages and potatoes over halfway through cooking. Add the bacon and tomatoes to the pan and bake for a further 5 minutes, until the potatoes are crisp and sausages cooked through. Using the back of a spoon, make 2 indentations in the potatoes. Crack an egg into each and season with salt and pepper. Return to the oven and bake for 3 to 4 minutes, until the eggs are softly set.

Carefully divide the mixture between 2 plates and serve immediately with tomato or steak sauce.

# spiralized zucchini egg rolls with smoked salmon and avocado

Using a spiralizer fitted with an ⅛-inch spaghetti blade, spiralize the zucchini. Coarsely snip any extra-long spirals in half with scissors. Place the spiralized zucchini on a clean dish cloth or paper towels and gently squeeze out any excess liquid.

In a small pitcher, lightly beat the eggs with salt and pepper.

Heat a small nonstick skillet over medium heat and spray or brush with oil. Add half the spiralized zucchini and stir-fry for 1 minute, then pour in half of the beaten eggs, swirling the skillet to coat the bottom. Cook for 2 to 3 minutes, then flip the omelet over and cook for a further minute until set.

Meanwhile, halve, seed, and peel the avocado and cut into strips.

Slide the omelet onto a board, add half the smoked salmon or trout and avocado, and roll up. Serve immediately. Repeat with the remaining ingredients to make 2 egg rolls.

**Serves 2**
**Prepare in 5 minutes**
**Cook in 8 to 10 minutes**

1 zucchini, ends trimmed and halved widthwise

3 eggs

cooking spray oil or a little sunflower oil, for frying

1 ripe avocado

4 slices smoked salmon or trout, cut into strips

salt and freshly ground black pepper

*A variation on a traditional British dish combining eggs, curry, and fish, this makes a perfect weekend breakfast or brunch.*

# smoked haddock and sweet potato kedgeree

**Serves 2**

**Prepare in 10 minutes**

**Cook in 10 to 12 minutes**

1 sweet potato, about 10 oz, peeled, ends trimmed, and halved widthwise

1 small onion, ends trimmed

2 teaspoons sunflower oil

1 tablespoon butter

1 tablespoon gluten-free mild or medium curry paste

7 oz boneless, skinless smoked haddock, cut into small chunks

½ cup frozen peas

juice of ½ lemon

2 eggs

2 tablespoons chopped flat-leaf parsley

salt and freshly ground black pepper

lemon wedges, to serve

Using a spiralizer fitted with an ⅛-inch spaghetti blade, spiralize the sweet potato. This should yield approximately ½ pound sweet potato spirals.

Place the spiralized sweet potato in a food processor and pulse until it resembles rice.

Spiralize the onion and snip the spirals into pieces 2 to 2½ inches long using scissors.

Heat the oil and butter in a large nonstick skillet or wok with a lid over medium heat. Add the spiralized onion and cook for 2 to 3 minutes, until softened. Stir in the sweet potato rice and curry paste and cook for a further 2 minutes, stirring to coat the rice in the paste. Stir in the haddock, peas, and lemon juice, cover, and cook over low heat for 5 to 6 minutes, until the fish is cooked through and the sweet potato rice is tender.

Meanwhile, bring a small saucepan of water to a boil, add the eggs, and cook for 4 minutes. Drain, let cool slightly, and then peel the shell off of the eggs.

Stir the parsley into the kedgeree and season to taste with salt and pepper. Cut the eggs into quarters.

Divide the kedgeree between 2 plates and top with the quartered eggs. Serve immediately with lemon wedges for squeezing.

*This colorful hash make a great weekend breakfast or brunch, and is full of nutritious nutrients.*

# beet, onion, and sweet potato hash

**Serves 2**
**Prepare in 10 minutes**
**Cook in 15 to 20 minutes**

1 red onion, ends trimmed

1 sweet potato, peeled, ends trimmed, and halved widthwise

1 fresh beet, scrubbed and ends trimmed

2 teaspoons olive oil, divided

4 oz chorizo sausage, diced

2 eggs

pinch of smoked paprika

1 tablespoon chopped flat-leaf parsley

salt and freshly ground black pepper

Using a spiralizer fitted with an ⅛-inch spaghetti blade, spiralize the onion and set it aside. Change to a ¼-inch flat noodle blade and spiralize the sweet potato and beet.

Heat 1 teaspoon of the oil in a large nonstick skillet or wok with a lid over medium heat. Add the chorizo and spiralized onion and cook for 2 to 3 minutes, until the onion has softened and the paprika oil has been released from the chorizo. Remove the mixture from the skillet.

Add the remaining oil to the skillet, stir in the spiralized beet and sweet potato, and stir-fry for 2 to 3 minutes. Then cover and let steam for 3 to 4 minutes, until just tender. Season to taste with salt and pepper.

Return the chorizo and onion to the skillet and mix well. Cook, uncovered, for 2 to 3 minutes, without stirring, until the bottom is lightly browned. Turn the mixture over and cook for a further 2 to 3 minutes. Using the back of a spoon, make 2 holes in the mixture. Crack in the eggs, cover, and cook for 3 to 4 minutes, until the eggs are just set.

Sprinkle with the paprika, scatter with the parsley, and serve immediately.

*If you don't have a Yorkshire pudding tray you can use a nonstick muffin caps pan and add about 5 minutes to the cooking time.*

# mini bacon, tomato, and ricotta frittatas

Lightly oil the holes of a nonstick 6-hole Yorkshire pudding tray. (Each hole should be about 4 inches in diameter.) Otherwise, use 6 holes of a muffin caps pan.

Heat the oil in a skillet over medium heat. Add the bacon and cook for 3 to 4 minutes, until lightly browned. Drain on paper towels.

Meanwhile, using a spiralizer fitted with an ⅛-inch spaghetti blade, spiralize the zucchini. Place the spiralized zucchini on a clean dish cloth or paper towels and gently squeeze out any excess liquid. Coarsely snip any really long spirals in half with scissors.

In a large bowl, beat together the eggs and chives and season with salt and pepper. Add the spiralized zucchini and the bacon and stir well.

Divide the mixture between the prepared holes, dot each with the ricotta, and add 2 tomato halves to each. Bake in a preheated oven at 350°F for 15 minutes, until set. Serve the frittatas warm. Any leftovers can be stored for up to 2 to 3 days in an airtight container in the refrigerator.

(gf) (lc)

**Makes 6**
**Prepare in 10 minutes**
**Cook in 20 minutes**

1 teaspoon olive oil, plus extra for greasing

3 slices smoked bacon, rind removed and discarded, chopped

1 zucchini, ends trimmed and halved widthwise

6 eggs

1 tablespoon snipped chives

2 oz ricotta cheese

6 cherry or baby plum tomatoes, halved

salt and freshly ground black pepper

# light bites

*Pho, pronounced "fuh" not "fo," is probably Vietnam's most famous dish. This fragrant soup is perfect for a light meal.*

# Vietnamese chicken pho with daikon noodles

(gf) (lc)

**Serves 2**
**Prepare in 10 minutes**
**Cook in 25 minutes**

2 teaspoons sunflower oil

1 teaspoon black peppercorns

1 lemongrass stalk, trimmed and sliced

½ cinnamon stick

1 star anise

1-inch piece fresh ginger root, peeled and thinly sliced

2½ cups hot gluten-free chicken stock

1⅔ cups boiling water

1 boneless, skinless chicken breast

9-oz piece daikon, peeled, ends trimmed, and halved widthwise

½ carrot, peeled and ends trimmed

2 teaspoons gluten-free Thai fish sauce

juice of 1 lime

3 scallions, thinly shredded

½ fat red chile, seeded and very thinly sliced

a small handful of cilantro leaves

2 lime wedges, to serve

Heat the oil in a large saucepan, add the peppercorns, lemon grass, cinnamon, star anise, and ginger and cook for 1 to 2 minutes to release their aromas. Add the stock, measurement water, and chicken breast. Bring to a boil, then cover and simmer for 20 minutes or until the chicken is cooked through.

Meanwhile, using a spiralizer fitted with an ⅛-inch spaghetti blade, spiralize the daikon and carrot, keeping them separate. This should yield about ½ pound spiralized daikon.

Remove the chicken from the stock and set aside. Strain the stock through a sieve into a pitcher and return it to the pan. Shred the chicken using 2 forks, then add to the stock. Stir in the fish sauce, lime juice, spiralized daikon, and the scallions. Cook for 3 minutes or until the noodles are tender.

Divide the pho between 2 bowls and scatter with the chile, spiralized carrot, and the cilantro. Serve immediately with lime wedges for squeezing.

*For a vegetarian soup, just omit the crispy bacon garnish and top with a little crumbled vegetarian cheese.*

# celery root and apple soup with bacon

**Serves 2**
**Prepare in 5 minutes**
**Cook in 15 to 20 minutes**

1 onion, ends trimmed

l lb celery root, peeled and cut into 5-inch chunks

1 tablespoon olive oil

1 tablespoon butter

2 eating apples, ends trimmed

1 small thyme sprig

3 cups hot gluten-free vegetable stock

salt and freshly ground black pepper

**For the crispy bacon garnish**

1 teaspoon olive oil

2 slices smoked Canadian bacon, chopped

6 sage leaves

Using a spiralizer fitted with an ⅛-inch spaghetti blade, spiralize the onion and celery root, keeping them separate.

Heat the oil and butter in a saucepan, add the spiralized onion, and cook over low heat for 2 to 3 minutes, until softened.

Meanwhile, spiralize the apples using the ⅛-inch spaghetti blade.

Add the spiralized celery root and apples to the pan and cook for 2 minutes, then add the thyme and stock. Bring to a boil, then reduce the heat, cover, and simmer for 10 to 12 minutes, until the celery root and apples are softened.

Carefully pour three-quarters of the soup into a large pitcher, then purée with a hand-held stick blender until smooth. Stir into the soup remaining in the pan, heat through, and season to taste.

Meanwhile, make the garnish. Heat the oil in a skillet over medium heat, add the bacon, and cook until colored, then stir in the sage leaves and cook until crispy.

Ladle the soup into 2 bowls and serve topped with the crispy bacon and sage.

*You can make your own sushi using vegetable rice. I've chosen daikon, but the rolls would also work with carrot or beet rice.*

# salmon, avocado, and daikon rice nori rolls

Line a small baking pan with paper towels.

Using a spiralizer fitted with an ⅛-inch spaghetti blade, spiralize the daikon. Place in a food processor and pulse until it resembles rice. Spread out the daikon rice in the prepared baking pan, place another piece of paper towel on top, and press down to absorb any excess liquid.

Place the mayonnaise and wasabi paste in a bowl, mix together, and season to taste with salt and pepper. Stir in the daikon rice.

Seed and peel the avocado, then cut into thin slices.

Place a sheet of nori on a bamboo mat, shiny-side down. Spread half of the daikon rice mixture evenly over the nori, leaving a border of about 1 inch at the top edge. Arrange half the salmon slices over the rice, then top with half the avocado slices in a single layer. Roll up the nori tightly from the bottom edge, using the mat to help form a tight roll. Place on a board, seam-side down. Repeat with the remaining ingredients to make 2 rolls.

Trim the ends of the rolls, then using a wet knife, slice each into 6 pieces. Serve with pickled ginger, extra wasabi, and soy sauce.

**Makes 12**
**Prepare in 15 minutes**

½-lb piece daikon, peeled, ends trimmed, and halved widthwise

2 tablespoons gluten-free light mayonnaise

1 teaspoon wasabi paste, plus extra to serve

½ ripe avocado

2 nori (dried seaweed) sheets

4 oz smoked salmon, cut into strips

salt and freshly ground black pepper

**To serve**
gluten-free pickled ginger
gluten-free soy sauce

*Serving this thin and crispy pizza is a great way of getting the kids to eat extra vegetables.*

# cauliflower-crust Mediterranean pizza

**Serves 2**
**Prepare in 10 minutes**
**Cook in 20 to 25 minutes**

**For the base**

1 lb 2 oz cauliflower florets

1 teaspoon dried oregano

½ teaspoon garlic salt

¼ cup grated vegetarian pasta cheese or Parmesan cheese

1 egg, beaten

salt and freshly ground black pepper

**For the topping**

½ zucchini, ends trimmed

2 tablespoons sun-dried tomato paste

¼ cup grated mozzarella cheese

½ yellow bell pepper, cored, seeded, and diced

6 cherry tomatoes, halved

3 oz soft goat cheese, coarsely chopped

basil leaves

Place a large nonstick cookie sheet in a preheated oven at 400°F.

Place the cauliflower in a food processor and pulse until it resembles rice. Transfer to a microwavable bowl, cover with plastic wrap, and pierce the top. Cook on full power in a microwave for 4 minutes, until tender. (Alternatively, cook in a steamer over a pan of boiling water.) Let cool slightly, then place in a clean dish cloth and squeeze over the sink to remove the excess liquid. Return to the bowl and add the oregano, garlic salt, vegetarian pasta cheese or Parmesan, egg, and salt and pepper. Mix well.

Transfer the mixture to a piece of nonstick parchment paper. Using your hands, flatten into a thin disk about 9 inches in diameter, then carefully transfer to the hot cookie sheet. Bake for 12 to 15 minutes, until golden brown.

Meanwhile, using a spiralizer fitted with a ribbon blade, spiralize the zucchini.

Spread the tomato paste over the pizza crust and scatter with the mozzarella. Top with the spiralized zucchini, yellow bell pepper, and tomatoes, and then dot with the goat cheese.

Return the pizza to the oven and bake for 5 to 7 minutes or until the vegetables are cooked through and the cheese is melted. Scatter with the basil and serve immediately.

*These Moroccan-style patties can be served with a crisp green salad as well as the creamy yogurt dip.*

# beet, chickpea, and rose harissa patties

**Serves 2**
**Prepare in 10 minutes**
**Cook in 8 to 10 minutes**

1 fresh beet, about 7 oz, scrubbed and ends trimmed

1 x 14 oz can chickpeas, drained and rinsed

2 tablespoons olive oil, plus extra for frying

2 teaspoons rose harissa paste

2 teaspoons tahini paste

2 teaspoons ground cumin

2 tablespoons coarsely chopped fresh cilantro

2 tablespoons buckwheat flour

salt and freshly ground black pepper

**For the dip**
¼ cup Greek yogurt

2 tablespoons chopped mint

1 teaspoon pomegranate molasses

½ teaspoon rose harissa paste

Using a spiralizer fitted with an ⅛-inch spaghetti blade, spiralize the beet.

Place the chickpeas in a food processor with the oil, harissa and tahini pastes, cumin, and cilantro and blend to a smooth paste. Add the spiralized beet and pulse a few times until the beet has broken down slightly.

Transfer the chickpea and beet mixture to a bowl, add the flour, and mix well. Season with salt and pepper and shape the mixture into 4 thick patties.

To make the dip, mix together all the ingredients in a bowl, season to taste, and set aside.

Heat a little oil in a large skillet over medium heat. Add the patties and cook for 4 to 5 minutes on each side, until golden brown and crisp. Serve the patties with the yogurt dip.

If you prefer, you can make 8 smaller patties and cook for just 3 to 4 minutes on each side.

*These Indian-inspired fritters are delicious served with a cooling cucumber dip or mango chutney.*

# spicy carrot and cilantro fritters

Using a spiralizer fitted with an ⅛-inch spaghetti blade, spiralize the carrots and onion.

In a large bowl, mix together the flour, baking powder, spices, and salt. Stir in the eggs and buttermilk or yogurt to make a smooth batter. Add the spiralized vegetables, the garlic, and cilantro and stir to combine.

Heat a little of the oil in a large nonstick skillet over medium heat. Cooking 4 fritters at a time, add heaped tablespoons of the batter to the skillet and flatten them slightly. Cook for 3 minutes on each side, until golden. Repeat until all the batter is used up. Serve the fritters with a cucumber dip and lemon wedges for squeezing on the side.

**Makes about 6**
**Prepare in 10 minutes**
**Cook in 15 minutes**

7 oz carrots, peeled, ends trimmed, and halved widthwise

1 small onion, ends trimmed

½ cup gram (chickpea) flour

1 teaspoon gluten-free baking powder

1 teaspoon ground cumin

1 teaspoon garam masala

½ teaspoon ground turmeric

½ teaspoon salt

2 eggs, lightly beaten

½ cup buttermilk or plain yogurt

1 garlic clove, crushed

2 tablespoons chopped fresh cilantro

1 tablespoon olive or sunflower oil, for frying

**To serve**
cucumber dip
lemon wedges

# smoky black bean, chipotle, and vegetable quesadilla

**Serves 2 to 3**
**Prepare in 5 minutes**
**Cook in 6 to 8 minutes**

1 carrot, peeled, ends trimmed, and halved widthwise

½ zucchini, ends trimmed

⅔ cup canned black beans, drained

2 tablespoons chipotle sauce

2 large soft flour tortillas

2 scallions, chopped

⅓ cup canned kernel corn

¾ cup grated mozzarella cheese

2 teaspoons olive oil

mixed salad, to serve

Using a spiralizer fitted with an ⅛-inch spaghetti blade, spiralize the carrot and zucchini.

In a small bowl, mash the beans with the chipotle sauce.

Lay out 1 tortilla on a board and spread with the black bean mixture, then top with the spiralized vegetables and scatter with the scallions, kernel corn, and cheese. Place the remaining tortilla on top and press down.

Brush a large nonstick skillet or griddle with the oil and place over medium heat. When hot, add the quesadilla and cook for 3 to 4 minutes, pressing down with a spatula until the cheese starts to melt and the quesadilla is golden underneath.

Place a large plate over the skillet or griddle and carefully invert the skillet or griddle to turn the quesadilla onto the plate. Return to the skillet or griddle and cook on the other side for 3 to 4 minutes, until golden.

Transfer the quesadilla to a board, cut into wedges, and serve with a mixed salad.

# kohlrabi carpaccio with Parma ham and Parmesan cheese

Using a spiralizer fitted with a ribbon blade, spiralize the kohlrabi.

Arrange the spiralized kohlrabi on a large plate, then sprinkle with the lemon juice and drizzle with the oil. Sprinkle with a little sea salt, some pepper, and the thyme and then let stand to marinate for about 1 hour.

Just before you are ready to serve, using a potato peeler, shave the piece of Parmesan over the dish and arrange the ham on top. Divide between 2 plates and serve immediately.

**Serves 2 as an appetizer**

**Prepare in 5 minutes, plus marinating**

1 small kohlrabi, peeled and ends trimmed

juice of ½ lemon

2 teaspoons olive oil

a few small lemon thyme sprigs

1 oz Parmesan cheese

4 slices Parma ham or prosciutto

sea salt and freshly ground black pepper

*This Thai-style salad is hot, fruity, and fragrant. It also works well with cooked peeled shrimp.*

# spicy crab and green papaya lettuce wraps

**Serves 4**

**Prepare in 15 minutes, plus marinating**

1 small green papaya, about 14½ oz, peeled and ends trimmed

1 carrot, peeled, ends trimmed, and halved widthwise

4 scallions, finely sliced

7 oz white crab meat

2 tablespoons chopped fresh cilantro

12 large Little Gem lettuce leaves

**For the dressing**

1 passion fruit

juice of 1 lime

1 teaspoon jaggery or soft brown sugar

2 teaspoons finely grated fresh ginger root

1 teaspoon gluten-free fish sauce

½ to 1 red chile, seeded and finely chopped

Cut the papaya in half widthwise and tap out the seeds. Attach the narrow end of one half of the papaya to a spiralizer fitted with an ⅛-inch spaghetti blade and spiralize. Repeat with the remaining papaya half. Place the spiralized papaya in a large bowl. Spiralize the carrot and add to the bowl along with the scallions.

To make the dressing, halve the passion fruit and, using a teaspoon, scoop out the pulp into a small bowl. Stir in the remaining dressing ingredients, adding the chopped chile to taste, and stir until the sugar has dissolved.

Add the crab to the papaya mixture and pour in half the dressing. Toss well and let stand to marinate for about 10 minutes, stirring halfway through the marinating time. Stir in the cilantro.

Place the lettuce leaves on a large plate and spoon some papaya and crab mixture into each leaf. Serve immediately with the remaining dressing in a small bowl on the side for drizzling.

*This Asian-inspired tuna salad is fresh and zingy and makes a perfect lunch or light evening meal.*

# griddled tuna with carrot and cucumber salad

**Serves 2**

**Prepare in 15 minutes, plus marinating**

**Cook in 4 to 6 minutes**

2 x 6 oz tuna steaks, about 1 inch thick

½ cucumber, ends trimmed and halved widthwise

1 carrot, peeled, ends trimmed, and halved widthwise

2 Little Gem lettuces, ends trimmed and each cut into quarters

4 scallions, thinly sliced

2 teaspoons toasted sesame seeds

**For the marinade**

finely grated zest and juice of 2 limes

¼ cup gluten-free soy sauce

1 garlic clove, crushed

2 teaspoons freshly grated ginger root

1 teaspoon sesame oil

2 teaspoons light brown sugar

In a small bowl, mix together the marinade ingredients and stir until the sugar has dissolved. Pour half into a shallow nonmetallic dish, reserving the remainder to use as a dressing. Add the tuna to the dish and turn it over to coat in the marinade. Let stand to marinate for about 15 minutes.

Meanwhile, using a spiralizer fitted with an ⅛-inch spaghetti blade, spiralize the cucumber and carrot.

Add the spiralized vegetables to a bowl with the lettuce and scallions.

Heat a griddle pan over high heat. Remove the tuna from the marinade, add to the pan, and cook for 2 to 3 minutes on each side or until the outside is cooked but the middle is still pink, brushing with any remaining marinade from the dish.

Drizzle the reserved dressing over the carrot and cucumber salad and toss well, then divide between 2 plates. Top the salad with the tuna steaks, scatter with the sesame seeds, and serve immediately.

*This spicy warming soup can be adapted to add whatever vegetables you have on hand.*

# winter vegetable and red lentil soup

Using a spiralizer fitted with an ⅛-inch spaghetti blade, spiralize all the vegetables, keeping the onion separate.

Heat the oil in a saucepan, add the spiralized onion, and cook over low heat for 3 to 4 minutes, until softened. Stir in the chile and cumin and cook for 1 minute, then stir in the lentils.

Add the stock and bring to a boil, then reduce the heat, cover, and simmer for 15 minutes, stirring occasionally, until the lentils are tender. Add all the remaining spiralized vegetables and simmer for a further 4 to 5 minutes or until the soup has thickened and the vegetables are tender. Season to taste.

Ladle the soup into bowls and serve with a dollop of yogurt and scattered with some chopped cilantro.

**Serves 2 to 3**
**Prepare in 10 minutes**
**Cook in 25 minutes**

1 onion, ends trimmed

1 sweet potato, peeled, ends trimmed, and halved widthwise

1 carrot, peeled, ends trimmed, and halved widthwise

1 parsnip, peeled, ends trimmed, and halved widthwise

1 tablespoon sunflower oil

1 red chile, seeded and chopped

1 tablespoon ground cumin

¼ cup red lentils, rinsed in cold water and drained

3 cups hot gluten-free vegetable stock

salt and freshly ground black pepper

**To serve**
Greek-style yogurt
chopped fresh cilantro

*This salad can be served as a light lunch. For a more substantial meal, serve this with some warm bread.*

# zucchini, tomato, and mozzarella salad

**Serves 4**

**Prepare in 10 minutes, plus marinating**

2 zucchini, ends trimmed, and halved widthwise

10 oz cherry or baby plum tomatoes, halved

2 tablespoons pitted black olives

1 x 8 oz ball buffalo mozzarella cheese, drained

3 tablespoons pine nuts, toasted

12 basil leaves

**For the dressing**

1 garlic clove, crushed

1 teaspoon aged balsamic vinegar

1 teaspoon capers, chopped

juice of 1 lemon

2 tablespoons olive oil

freshly ground black pepper

Using a spiralizer fitted with a ribbon blade, spiralize the zucchini. Coarsely snip any extra-long ribbons in half with a pair of scissors.

Place the spiralized zucchini in a large bowl and add the tomatoes and olives.

To make the dressing, beat together all the dressing ingredients in a small bowl. Pour the dressing over the salad, reserving a little, then let stand to marinate for about 10 minutes.

Place the zucchini, tomatoes, and olives on a platter. Tear the mozzarella into pieces and arrange them on the salad, then scatter with the pine nuts and basil leaves. Drizzle with the remaining dressing and serve immediately.

*These crispy strings are perfect for munching on as a snack or for serving with drinks.*

# Marmite and cheese potato strings

Line a large baking pan with nonstick parchment paper.

Using a spiralizer fitted with an ⅛-inch spaghetti blade, spiralize the potatoes. Coarsely snip the spirals into 5- to 6-inch pieces using scissors.

Place the spiralized potatoes in a large bowl, add 2 teaspoons of the oil, and season with a little pepper. Toss the strings to coat in the oil and seasoning.

Spread out the spiralized potatoes in a single layer in the prepared baking pan and bake in a preheated oven at 400°F for 10 minutes.

Meanwhile, in a large bowl, mix together the Marmite, remaining oil, and the cheese.

Remove the strings from the oven and toss in the Marmite mixture, stirring until evenly coated. Return to the oven and bake for a further 10 to 12 minutes, until crispy, turning them over once. (Remove any strings that are already cooked when you turn the potatoes over.) Remove from the oven and let cool. The strings can be stored for up to 2 to 3 days in an airtight container.

**Serves 4 as a snack**
**Prepare in 5 minutes**
**Cook in 20 to 22 minutes**

2 potatoes, skins scrubbed and ends trimmed

1 tablespoon sunflower oil, divided

1 tablespoon Marmite or yeast extract

¼ cup finely grated sharp Cheddar cheese

freshly ground black pepper

*This pretty salad combines crunch from the apples and fennel with tangy blue cheese.*

# apple, fennel, and Gorgonzola salad

First, make the dressing. In a small bowl, beat together all the dressing ingredients and season to taste with a little salt and pepper.

Using a spiralizer fitted with a ribbon blade, spiralize the fennel and apples. Snip any really long ribbons into shorter pieces with scissors.

Place the spiralized fennel and apples in a bowl and drizzle with half the dressing. Add the radishes and toss gently to coat.

Divide the pea shoots or watercress among 4 plates or arrange on a platter, then add the apple and fennel mixture. Scatter the salad with the walnuts, cheese pieces, and chopped fennel tops. Drizzle with the remaining dressing and serve immediately.

(gf) (lc)

**Serves 4**
**Prepare in 10 minutes**

1 large fennel bulb, ends trimmed and leafy tops chopped

1 large red eating apple, ends trimmed

1 large green eating apple, ends trimmed

1 ¼ cups thinly sliced radishes

3 oz pea shoots or watercress

½ cup walnut halves

4 oz Gorgonzola cheese, broken into small pieces

**For the dressing**

2 tablespoons extra virgin olive oil

2 tablespoons apple cider vinegar

2 teaspoons gluten-free wholegrain mustard

2 teaspoons honey

salt and freshly ground black pepper

*This hearty soup, flavored with warming spices, is perfect for a fall or winter's day meal.*

# spiced butternut squash, potato, and chorizo soup

**Serves 4**
**Prepare in 10 minutes**
**Cook in 20 minutes**

1 large onion, ends trimmed

1 potato, peeled and ends trimmed

½ butternut squash (the non-bulbous end), about 1 lb, peeled and halved widthwise

1 tablespoon olive oil

½ teaspoon ground cinnamon

1 teaspoon ground ginger

pinch of ground nutmeg

3 cups hot gluten-free chicken or vegetable stock

4 oz chorizo, diced

salt and freshly ground black pepper

1 tablespoon snipped chives, to garnish

Using a spiralizer fitted with an ⅛-inch spaghetti blade, spiralize the onion and set it aside. Change to a ¼-inch flat noodle blade and spiralize the potato and squash.

Heat the oil in a large saucepan, add the spiralized onion, and cook over medium heat for 3 to 4 minutes, stirring occasionally, until softened. Stir in the spiralized potato and squash, cover, and cook for 3 minutes.

Stir in the spices and cook for 1 minute, then add the stock. Cover and let simmer for 10 minutes or until the potatoes and squash are tender. Transfer half the soup to a food processor or blender and blend in batches until smooth. Return to the pan and reheat gently. Season to taste with salt and pepper.

Meanwhile, heat a nonstick skillet over medium heat, add the chorizo, and cook for 2 to 3 minutes, stirring occasionally, until the paprika oil has been released from the chorizo and it is crispy.

Ladle the soup into 4 bowls, top with the chorizo and chives, and serve immediately.

*These crunchy zucchini and cheese chips make a great snack or accompaniment to a glass of wine.*

# oven-baked zucchini and cheese chips

Line 2 large baking pans with nonstick parchment paper.

Using a spiralizer fitted with a ribbon blade, spiralize the zucchini. Snip the spirals into 3-inch pieces with scissors.

Place the polenta, vegetarian pasta cheese or Parmesan, and pepper in a bowl and mix together to combine. In a separate small bowl, whisk the egg whites with a fork until frothy. Place the spiralized zucchini, a few at a time, into the egg whites and toss them very gently to coat. Then place in the cheese mixture and gently shake until completely coated in the mixture.

Transfer the zucchini to the prepared baking pans, leaving a small space between each spiral. Sprinkle them with any remaining cheese mixture and bake in a preheated oven at 400°F for 12 to 15 minutes, turning once, until crisp. Serve immediately.

**Serves 2**
**Prepare in 10 minutes**
**Cook in 12 to 15 minutes**

1 zucchini, ends trimmed and halved widthwise

½ cup fine polenta (cornmeal)

½ cup finely grated vegetarian pasta cheese or Parmesan cheese

2 egg whites

freshly ground black pepper

# chicken with beet rice, pomegranate, and pistachio tabbouleh

**Serves 2**

**Prepare in 15 minutes, plus marinating**

**Cook in 8 to 12 minutes**

2 teaspoons grated orange zest, divided

¼ cup orange juice, divided

2 tablespoons olive oil, divided

2 tablespoons pomegranate molasses, divided

2 boneless, skinless chicken breasts

2 fresh beets, scrubbed and ends trimmed

¼ cup chopped flat-leaf parsley

¼ cup chopped mint

2 oz baby kale or spinach

1 cup pomegranate seeds

3 tablespoons pistachio nuts

salt and freshly ground black pepper

In a large nonmetallic bowl, mix together half of the orange zest, orange juice, oil, and pomegranate molasses. Add the chicken breasts and let stand to marinate for about 15 minutes.

Meanwhile, using a spiralizer fitted with an ⅛-inch spaghetti blade, spiralize the beet. Place the spiralized beet in a food processor and pulse until it resembles rice.

Pour the beet rice into a large bowl and stir in the herbs, kale or spinach, pomegranate seeds, and pistachio nuts.

In a separate small bowl, mix together the remaining orange zest, orange juice, oil, and pomegranate molasses. Season to taste with salt and pepper, then pour evenly over the beet tabbouleh and toss well.

Heat a griddle pan until hot. Add the chicken and cook over medium heat for 4 to 6 minutes on each side or until cooked through, basting occasionally.

Divide the tabbouleh between 2 bowls. Thinly slice the chicken, arrange it on top, and serve immediately.

*This Korean dish is made by fermenting Chinese leaves, carrot, and daikon. It's a great accompaniment to meat and fish dishes.*

# easy spiralized vegetable kimchi

**Makes 1 x 2-pint jar**

**Prepare in 15 minutes, plus overnight standing and fermenting**

1 small napa cabbage, quartered lengthwise and cut into 1-inch strips

2 tablespoons sea salt

2 carrots, peeled, ends trimmed, and halved widthwise

5-oz piece daikon, peeled, ends trimmed, and halved widthwise

4 scallions, chopped

**For the kimchi paste**

1-inch piece fresh ginger root, peeled and grated

2 garlic cloves, crushed

¼ cup rice vinegar

1 tablespoon gluten-free Thai fish sauce

2 tablespoons gluten-free sriracha chili sauce or chile paste

1 teaspoon superfine sugar

Place the napa cabbage leaves in a bowl, add the sea salt, and mix together. Let stand for 4 to 5 hours or overnight.

Using a spiralizer fitted with an ⅛-inch spaghetti blade, spiralize the carrots and daikon.

Place the spiralized vegetables in a large bowl with the scallions. Rinse the napa cabage leaves under cold running water, drain, dry thoroughly, and then add to the bowl.

To make the kimchi paste, place all the ingredients in a small bowl and blend together. Stir the paste into the vegetables until evenly coated.

Pack the vegetable mixture into a large jar or freezer box, seal, and let ferment at room temperature overnight. Transfer to the refrigerator and use within 2 weeks. The flavor will improve the longer it's left in the fridge.

*Use a golden beet, if you can find one. If you use a red beet, it will stain the pickle red.*

# mixed vegetable ribbon pickle

(gf) (lc) (v) (vg)

**Serves 4**

**Prepare in 10 minutes, plus salting and marinating**

1 carrot, peeled, ends trimmed, and halved widthwise

1 cucumber, ends trimmed, and cut into 4 pieces widthwise

1 fresh golden beet, scrubbed and ends trimmed

1 cup thinly sliced radishes

2 tablespoons sea salt flakes

1 cup white wine vinegar

⅓ cup superfine sugar

½ cup water

1 teaspoon yellow mustard seeds

2 teaspoons fennel seeds

¼ cup coarsely chopped dill

Using a spiralizer fitted with a ribbon blade, spiralize the carrot, cucumber, and beet.

Place the spiralized vegetables in a colander placed over a bowl, add the radish slices, and sprinkle with the salt. Toss to combine, then let stand for 20 minutes. Rinse under cold running water, then drain well.

Place the vinegar, sugar, and measurement water in a large jar or nonmetallic bowl and stir until the sugar has dissolved. Add the mustard and fennel seeds and dill. Stir in the drained vegetables and seal the jar or cover the bowl. Chill in the refrigerator for at least 20 minutes before serving.

*These pretty pickled cucumber spirals are quick to prepare and make an ideal accompaniment to cold meats or cheese.*

# pickled cucumber and dill spirals

Using a spiralizer fitted with a ribbon blade, spiralize the cucumber. Dry the spiralized cucumber on paper towels.

Place the vinegar, measurement water, sugar, and salt in a nonmetallic bowl and beat together until the sugar and salt have dissolved. Stir in the dill, garlic, and peppercorns.

Place the spiralized cucumber in a 1½-pint pickling jar with a lid. Pour in the vinegar mixture and stir well.

Seal the jar and let stand in the refrigerator for at least 1 day before serving. The pickled cucumber will keep for up to a few weeks in the refrigerator.

**Serves 6 to 8**

**Prepare in 10 minutes, plus 1 day pickling**

1 cucumber, ends trimmed and cut into 4 pieces widthwise

⅔ cup white wine vinegar

1¼ cups warm water

1 teaspoon superfine sugar

2 teaspoons sea salt

1 oz dill, coarsely chopped

4 garlic cloves, peeled and smashed

1 teaspoon black peppercorns

# mains

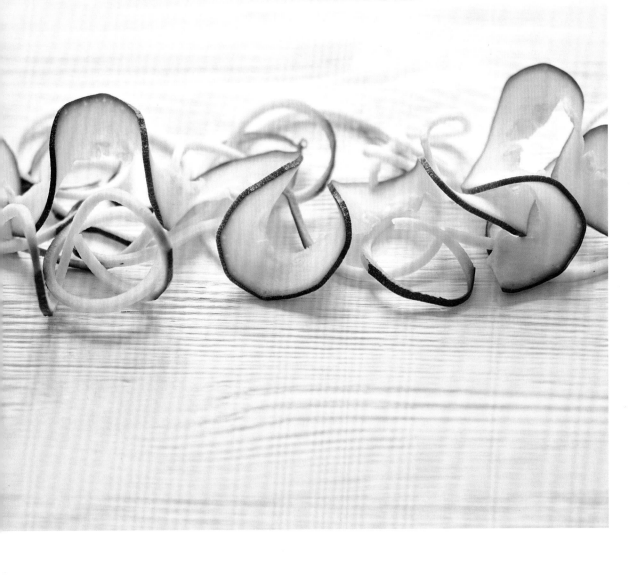

*The dumplings are served on a bed of carrot and zucchini spaghetti with a tangy chile and lime dressing.*

# Asian steamed chicken dumplings

**Serves 2**

**Prepare in 15 minutes**

**Cook in 15 minutes**

2 zucchini, ends trimmed and halved widthwise

1 carrot, peeled, ends trimmed, and halved widthwise

2 tablespoons toasted peanuts, coarsely chopped

finely grated zest and juice of 1 lime

⅓ cup gluten-free sweet chili sauce

½ teaspoon gluten-free Thai fish sauce

**For the dumplings**

2 scallions, coarsely chopped

1-inch piece fresh ginger root, peeled and chopped

1 red chile, seeded and chopped

1 small bunch of fresh cilantro

1 large boneless, skinless chicken breast, about 7 oz, cut into chunks

1 teaspoon gluten-free light soy sauce

First, make the dumplings. Place the scallions, ginger, chile, and cilantro in a food processor and blend until finely chopped. Add the chicken and soy sauce and pulse again until combined. Transfer the mixture to a bowl and shape into 12 small balls, using wet hands.

Place the dumplings in a steamer set over a pan of simmering water and steam for about 15 minutes or until cooked through.

Meanwhile, using a spiralizer fitted with an ⅛-inch spaghetti blade, spiralize the zucchini and carrot.

Place the spiralized vegetables in a bowl with the peanuts. Mix together the lime zest and juice, sweet chili sauce, and fish sauce in a separate small bowl, then pour it onto the zucchini and carrot, reserving a little. Stir well to coat the vegetables in the dressing.

Divide the vegetables between 2 plates and top with the dumplings. Drizzle with the reserved dressing and serve immediately.

# baked salmon, potato, and fennel parcels

**Serves 2**
**Prepare in 10 minutes**
**Cook in 15 minutes**

1 large potato, skin scrubbed, ends trimmed, and halved widthwise

½ fennel bulb, ends trimmed

2 teaspoons olive oil

1 tablespoon chopped parsley

6 pitted black olives

8 capers

6 plum or cherry tomatoes, halved

4 lemon wedges

2 skinless salmon fillets, about 7 oz each

salt and freshly ground black pepper

Using a spiralizer fitted with an ⅛-inch spaghetti blade, spiralize the potato and fennel. Coarsely snip any really long spirals of potato in half with scissors.

Transfer the spiralized vegetables to a bowl, add the oil and parsley, season well with salt and pepper, and mix together.

Place 2 x 9-inch squares of nonstick parchment paper on a large baking pan. Divide the potato and fennel mixture, olives, capers, tomatoes, and lemon wedges between the 2 squares of paper and then place a salmon fillet on top of each pile of vegetables. Fold the paper over to seal the parcels.

Place the baking pan in a preheated oven at 400°F for 15 minutes, until the salmon is opaque and flakes easily and the potatoes are tender. Transfer the parcels to plates. Carefully open the paper and squeeze some lemon juice onto the salmon. Serve immediately.

# beet, quinoa, and feta burgers with yogurt and harissa

Using a spiralizer fitted with an ⅛-inch spaghetti blade, spiralize the beet and carrot. Coarsely snip any long spirals in half with scissors.

Place the spiralized vegetables in a bowl, add the quinoa, walnuts, mint, lemon juice, harissa paste, flour, and feta and stir together. Mix in the egg and season well with salt and pepper. Transfer the mixture to a plate, cover, and let chill in the fridge for 30 minutes.

Divide the mixture into 4 portions and shape into burgers, using your hands. Place the burgers on a nonstick broiler pan and brush with a little oil. Cook the burgers under a preheated hot broiler for 6 to 7 minutes on each side or until cooked through.

Top the burgers with spoonfuls of yogurt drizzled with the harissa and serve with salad leaves and tomatoes.

**Makes 4**

**Prepare in 10 minutes, plus chilling**

**Cook in 12 to 15 minutes**

1 fresh beet, scrubbed and ends trimmed

1 carrot, peeled, ends trimmed, and halved widthwise

¾ cup cooked quinoa

½ cup chopped walnuts

¼ cup chopped mint

juice of ½ lemon

2 teaspoons harissa paste

2 tablespoons wholemeal flour

1 cup crumbled feta cheese

1 large egg, beaten

salt and freshly ground black pepper

1 tablespoon sunflower oil, for brushing

**To serve**

Greek-style yogurt

1 teaspoon harissa paste

mixed salad leaves and tomatoes

*Biryani is traditionally a rice dish. Here I have replaced the rice with low-carb cauliflower rice, which absorbs the spices well.*

# vegetable biryani with cauliflower rice

**Serves 4**
**Prepare in 10 minutes**
**Cook in 10 minutes**

1 lb 2 oz cauliflower florets

1 small onion, ends trimmed

1 large carrot, peeled, ends trimmed, and halved widthwise

1 zucchini, ends trimmed and halved widthwise

1 tablespoon sunflower oil

2 teaspoons black mustard seeds

5 cardamom pods, crushed

2 tablespoons gluten-free medium curry powder

1 cinnamon stick

6 curry leaves

1-inch piece fresh ginger root, peeled and finely grated

1 green chile, seeded and finely chopped

1 garlic clove, crushed

⅔ cup hot gluten-free vegetable stock or water, divided

2 tomatoes, chopped

salt and freshly ground black pepper

**To serve**

2 tablespoons chopped fresh cilantro

3 tablespoons toasted almonds

Place the cauliflower in a food processor and pulse until it resembles rice. Set aside.

Using a spiralizer fitted with an ⅛-inch spaghetti blade, spiralize the onion and set it aside. Change to a ribbon blade and spiralize the carrot and zucchini. Coarsely snip any long ribbons in half with scissors.

Heat the oil in a large skillet or wok over medium heat. Stir in the spices and curry leaves and cook for 1 minute or until the mustard seeds start to pop. Stir in the spiralized onion, the ginger, chile, garlic, and 2 tablespoons of the stock or water and cook for 3 to 4 minutes, until the onion has softened.

Add the cauliflower rice and stir to coat in the spices, then add the spiralized carrot and zucchini and the tomatoes. Stir well, then add the remaining stock or water. Cook for 5 minutes or until the liquid has evaporated and the rice and vegetables are tender, stirring occasionally. Season to taste with salt and pepper.

Divide the biryani among 4 bowls and scatter with the cilantro and almonds. Serve immediately.

# smoked salmon, zucchini, and dill crustless quiche

gf · lc

**Serves 4**
**Prepare in 10 minutes**
**Cook in 35 to 40 minutes**

1 zucchini, ends trimmed and halved widthwise

1 tablespoon sunflower oil, plus extra for greasing

4 eggs

1 ¼ cups reduced-fat crème fraîche, plus extra to serve

5 oz smoked salmon, cut into strips

¾ cup grated reduced-fat sharp Cheddar cheese

2 tablespoons chopped dill, plus extra sprigs to garnish

salt and freshly ground black pepper

watercress, to serve

Using a spiralizer fitted with a ribbon blade, spiralize the zucchini. Snip any extra-long ribbons into shorter pieces using scissors.

Place the spiralized zucchini in a bowl, add the oil, and toss to coat. Heat a large griddle pan until hot. Add the zucchini in a single layer and cook for 2 to 3 minutes, until lightly charred (you may need to do this in 2 batches). Transfer the zucchini to a plate lined with paper towels and let cool.

Lightly grease an 8-inch nonstick cake pan and line the bottom with nonstick parchment paper.

In a large bowl, lightly beat together the eggs and crème fraîche and then lightly season with salt and pepper. Add half the salmon and zucchini ribbons, ½ cup of the cheese, and the dill.

Pour into the prepared pan, top with the remaining zucchini and salmon, and scatter with the remaining cheese. Bake in a preheated oven at 350°F for 30 to 35 minutes or until the filling is just set. Remove from the oven and let cool slightly.

Cut the quiche into wedges, garnish with dill sprigs, and serve with large handfuls of watercress.

*These cheesy carrot tortillas are lower in carbs than traditional tortillas made from wheat flour.*

# carrot tortillas with chipotle chicken

Line 2 large baking pans with nonstick parchment paper.

First, make the tortillas. Using a spiralizer fitted with an ⅛-inch spaghetti blade, spiralize the carrots. Place the spiralized carrots in a steamer set over a pan of boiling water and steam for 3 minutes, until just tender. Let cool slightly, then place the carrots on a clean dish cloth or paper towels and gently squeeze out any excess liquid.

Add the carrots to a bowl, stir in all the remaining tortilla ingredients, and season well. Place 4 large, separate spoonfuls of the mixture onto the prepared baking pans and, using the back of a spoon, press out into thin disks about 6 inches in diameter. Bake in a preheated oven at 400°F for 10 minutes, until golden and crispy on the edges.

Meanwhile, heat the oil in a wok or large skillet. Add the chicken and stir-fry for 3 to 4 minutes, until browned. Add the onion and bell peppers and stir-fry for 2 to 3 minutes, then add the tomatoes and chipotle paste. Simmer for 5 minutes or until the sauce is thick and glossy, adding more chipotle paste to taste, if liked.

Divide the chipotle chicken between the warm tortillas, scatter with the cilantro, roll up, and serve immediately.

**Serves 2**
**Prepare in 15 minutes**
**Cook in 15 minutes**

2 teaspoons sunflower oil

2 small boneless, skinless chicken breasts, cut into thin strips

1 small red onion, sliced

½ red bell pepper, seeded and cut into thin strips

½ yellow bell pepper, seeded and cut into thin strips

1 x 8 oz can diced tomatoes

1 tablespoon chipotle paste, or to taste

2 tablespoons chopped fresh cilantro

### For the tortillas

2 large carrots, peeled, ends trimmed, and halved widthwise

2 eggs, beaten

¾ cup grated Cheddar cheese

2 tablespoons almond flour

salt and freshly ground black pepper

# jumbo shrimp with daikon noodles and Asian pesto

**Serves 2**

**Prepare in 10 minutes**

**Cook in 4 to 6 minutes**

1 daikon, about ¾ lb, peeled, ends trimmed, and halved widthwise

1 tablespoon peanut oil

7 oz raw peeled jumbo shrimp

**For the pesto**

1 lemon grass stalk, tough outer layers removed and discarded, coarsely chopped

1 small red chile, seeded and coarsely chopped

finely grated zest and juice of 1 lime

1 oz fresh cilantro

12 basil leaves

1-inch piece fresh ginger root, peeled and chopped

1 garlic clove

3 tablespoons gluten-free dry-roasted peanuts

2 tablespoons peanut oil

1 teaspoon gluten-free Thai fish sauce

First, make the pesto. Place all the pesto ingredients except the oil and fish sauce in a food processor and blitz to make a paste (you may need to scrape the mixture down the sides of the food processor with a rubber spatula from time to time). With the motor still running, gradually add the oil and fish sauce through the funnel until combined. Set aside.

Using a spiralizer fitted with an ⅛-inch spaghetti blade, spiralize the daikon.

Heat the oil in a large wok or skillet, add the shrimp, and cook for 2 to 3 minutes, until they have turned pink. Add the spiralized daikon and stir-fry for 2 to 3 minutes, until just tender. Stir in the pesto and toss well to coat the daikon noodles and shrimp. Serve immediately.

*If you prefer, you can just stir this nutrient-packed creamy sauce into raw spiralized zucchini.*

# zucchini spaghetti with herby avocado sauce

Using a spiralizer fitted with an ⅛-inch spaghetti blade, spiralize the zucchini.

Halve, seed, and peel the avocado, then place in a food processor with the garlic, lemon juice, herbs, and olive or avocado oil and blend until smooth. Season to taste with salt and pepper.

Spray a nonstick skillet or wok with spray oil and place over medium heat. Add the spiralized zucchini and stir-fry for 3 to 4 minutes, until just tender. Remove from the heat and stir in the sauce to coat.

Divide the spiralized zucchini between 2 bowls, scatter with the pine nuts and extra pepper, and serve immediately.

**Serves 2**
**Prepare in 10 minutes**
**Cook in 5 minutes**

2 zucchini, ends trimmed and halved widthwise

1 ripe avocado

1 garlic clove

juice of ½ lemon

¼ cup coarsely chopped flat-leaf parsley

1 oz basil leaves

2 tablespoons olive or avocado oil

cooking spray oil, for frying

3 tablespoons pine nuts, toasted

salt and freshly ground black pepper

*Give this classic Chinese dish a low-carb makeover by swapping egg noodles with carrot and daikon noodles.*

# chicken chow mein with vegetable noodles

In a large bowl, mix together 1 tablespoon each of the soy sauce, sherry or Chinese cooking wine, and oyster sauce, the sesame oil, and 1 teaspoon of the cornstarch. Add the chicken, stir to coat in the marinade, then cover and let marinate in the refrigerator for 20 minutes.

In a small bowl, mix together the remaining soy sauce, sherry or Chinese cooking wine, oyster sauce, and cornstarch and set aside.

Using a spiralizer fitted with a ¼-inch flat noodle blade, spiralize the carrot, keeping it separate. Change to an ⅛-inch spaghetti blade and spiralize the daikon.

Heat the sunflower oil in a wok or large skillet over high heat until hot. Add the chicken and stir-fry for 3 to 4 minutes, until lightly browned. Add the garlic, ginger, and scallions and stir-fry for 2 to 3 minutes. Add the spiralized vegetables and the snow peas and stir-fry for a further 3 to 4 minutes, until the vegetables are just tender and the chicken is cooked through. Add the bean sprouts and reserved sauce and stir until the sauce has thickened and all the ingredients are coated. Serve immediately.

**Serves 4**

**Prepare in 10 minutes, plus marinating**

**Cook in 10 to 15 minutes**

2 tablespoons gluten-free light soy sauce, divided

2 tablespoons dry sherry or Chinese cooking wine (Shaoxing), divided

3 tablespoons gluten-free oyster sauce, divided

½ teaspoon toasted sesame oil

2 teaspoons cornstarch, divided

3 boneless, skinless chicken breasts, cut into thin strips

1 large carrot, peeled, ends trimmed, and halved widthwise

1 daikon, about 1 lb, peeled, ends trimmed, and halved widthwise

1 tablespoon sunflower oil

1 garlic clove, crushed

2 teaspoons grated fresh ginger root

1 bunch of scallions, sliced

4 oz snow peas

1¼ cups bean sprouts

*This Bolognese will become a family favorite and is packed full of vegetables and flavor.*

# skinny turkey Bolognese with zucchini spaghetti

**Serves 4**
**Prepare in 10 minutes**
**Cook in 25 to 35 minutes**

3 zucchini (ideally yellow zucchini), ends trimmed and halved widthwise

1 large onion, ends trimmed

1 large carrot, peeled, ends trimmed, and halved widthwise

14½ oz lean ground turkey

1 garlic clove, crushed

3½ cups sliced white or cremini mushrooms

1 teaspoon paprika

⅔ cup red wine or gluten-free beef stock

1 x 14 oz can diced tomatoes

1 tablespoon tomato paste

2 teaspoons dried mixed herbs

salt and freshly ground black pepper

freshly grated Parmesan cheese, to serve

Using a spiralizer fitted with an ⅛-inch spaghetti blade, spiralize the zucchini and onion, keeping them separate. Change to a ribbon blade and spiralize the carrot. Coarsely snip any really long ribbons in half with scissors.

Place the ground turkey, spiralized onion, and garlic in a large nonstick saucepan and dry-fry over high heat for 3 to 4 minutes, until lightly browned. Stir in the spiralized carrot, mushrooms, and paprika and cook for 2 to 3 minutes. Stir in the red wine or stock and cook for 2 to 3 minutes, until the liquid has reduced, then stir in the tomatoes, tomato paste, and mixed herbs. Reduce the heat, cover, and let simmer for 15 to 20 minutes, stirring occasionally, until the sauce has reduced and thickened.

Season to taste with salt and pepper, then stir in the zucchini spaghetti and cook, uncovered, for 2 to 3 minutes or until the zucchini spaghetti is al dente. Serve sprinkled with a little freshly grated Parmesan.

# fennel and cauliflower risotto with lemon and arugula

**Serves 2**

**Prepare in 10 minutes**

**Cook in 10 to 15 minutes**

1 fennel bulb, ends trimmed and reserved

½ lb cauliflower florets

1 tablespoon olive oil

1 garlic clove, crushed

½ red chile, seeded and finely chopped (optional)

½ cup white wine

1 cup hot gluten-free vegetable stock

finely grated zest and juice of 1 small lemon

½ cup grated vegetarian pasta cheese or Parmesan cheese, plus extra to serve

2 tablespoons reduced-fat cream cheese

2½ cups arugula

salt and freshly ground black pepper

Using a spiralizer fitted with a ¼-inch flat noodle blade, spiralize the fennel.

Cut the trimmed ends of the fennel into small pieces and place in a food processor with the spiralized fennel and cauliflower florets. Pulse until the mixture resembles rice.

Heat the oil in a large skillet or wok, add the garlic and chile, if using, and cook over medium heat for 1 minute, until softened, then add the cauliflower and fennel rice. Stir-fry for 2 to 3 minutes, then pour in the wine and cook for 2 to 3 minutes until the liquid has reduced. Add half the stock and cook until most of the stock has evaporated. Stir in the remaining stock and half of the lemon zest and juice and season with salt and pepper. Cook for a further 2 to 3 minutes, until the rice is just tender.

Stir in the vegetarian pasta cheese or Parmesan, cream cheese, and most of the arugula, reserving a little. Cook for a further 1 to 2 minutes or until the arugula has wilted and the rice is tender. Stir in the remaining lemon zest and juice.

Divide the risotto between 2 bowls, top with the reserved arugula, and sprinkle with extra vegetarian pasta cheese or Parmesan and pepper. Serve immediately.

*Make this crowd pleaser into a low-carb meal with daikon noodles and plenty of vegetables.*

# sweet and sour pork with daikon noodles

Using a spiralizer fitted with a ¼-inch flat noodle blade, spiralize the carrot. Change to an ⅛-inch spaghetti blade and spiralize the daikon. Set the vegetables aside.

Drain the pineapple and pour the juice into a small bowl, reserving the pineapple pieces. Add all the sauce ingredients, except the cornstarch, to the pineapple juice and mix well. Place the cornstarch in a cup, then blend with 2 tablespoons of the sauce, stirring until smooth. Stir the cornstarch mixture into the sauce in the bowl.

Heat the oil in a wok or large skillet, add the pork, ginger, and garlic and stir-fry over high heat for 3 to 4 minutes until browned. Add the spiralized vegetables, red bell pepper, scallions, and reserved pineapple pieces and cook for a further 2 to 3 minutes, until the vegetables are tender and the pork is cooked through.

Pour the sauce mixture into the wok or skillet, bring to a boil, stirring continuously, and simmer for 2 to 3 minutes, until thickened. Serve immediately.

**Serves 4**
**Prepare in 15 minutes**
**Cook in 8 to 12 minutes**

1 carrot, peeled, ends trimmed, and halved widthwise

1 daikon, about 1 lb, peeled, ends trimmed, and halved widthwise

1 x 8 oz can pineapple pieces in natural juice

2 teaspoons sunflower oil

14½ oz pork fillet, cut into small cubes

2 teaspoons grated fresh ginger root

1 garlic clove, crushed

1 red bell pepper, cored, seeded, and cubed

1 bunch of scallions, sliced

**For the sauce**

1 tablespoon gluten-free tomato ketchup

1 tablespoon tomato paste

1 tablespoon gluten-free light soy sauce

2 tablespoons rice wine vinegar

1 tablespoon cornstarch

# butternut squash spaghetti with walnut and arugula pesto

**Serves 4**

**Prepare in 10 minutes**

**Cook in 10 minutes**

½ large butternut squash (the non-bulbous end), peeled and cut in half widthwise

2 teaspoons olive oil

freshly ground black pepper

**For the pesto**

3 ¾ cups arugula, plus extra to garnish

1 garlic clove

½ cup walnut halves

¼ cup grated vegetarian pasta cheese or Parmesan cheese

juice of ½ lemon

¼ cup extra virgin olive oil

First, make the pesto. Place the arugula, garlic, walnuts, vegetarian pasta cheese or Parmesan, and lemon juice in a food processor and blend until finely chopped (you may need to scrape the mixture down the sides of the food processor with a rubber spatula from time to time). With the motor still running, gradually add the oil through the funnel until combined.

Using a spiralizer fitted with an ⅛-inch spaghetti blade, spiralize the squash. This should yield about 1 pound of spiralized squash.

Heat the olive oil in a large wok or skillet, add the spiralized squash, and stir-fry for about 5 to 7 minutes, until softened but not broken up. Stir in the pesto until the squash spaghetti is well coated. Sprinkle with pepper, garnish with some arugula, and serve immediately.

# miso-baked cod with daikon noodles and Asian greens

(lc)

**Serves 2**

**Prepare in 15 minutes, plus marinating**

**Cook in 14 to 17 minutes**

2 chunky cod loins, about
   7 oz each

sunflower oil, for oiling

½ lb piece daikon, peeled, ends
   trimmed, and halved widthwise

3 tablespoons black sesame seeds

½ teaspoon superfine sugar

1 tablespoon seasoned soy sauce

1 tablespoon liquid dashi

1 teaspoon yuzu juice or lemon
   juice

10 oz choy sum and bok choy,
   stems trimmed and leaves cut
   into bite-size pieces

**For the marinade**

2 tablespoons white miso paste

3 tablespoons sake

1 garlic clove, crushed

1-inch piece fresh ginger root,
   peeled and finely grated

1 tablespoon superfine sugar

2 teaspoons mirin

In a shallow dish, mix together all the marinade ingredients, add the cod, and turn it over in the marinade to coat. Cover and let marinate in the refrigerator for 2 to 3 hours, or overnight

Lightly oil a baking pan. Using a spiralizer fitted with a ¼-inch flat noodle blade, spiralize the daikon.

Place the fish on the prepared baking pan and drizzle 1 tablespoon of the marinade over it. Bake in a preheated oven at 350°F for 10 to 12 minutes.

Preheat the broiler to high. Remove the fish from the oven, drizzle the remaining marinade over the fish, and broil for about 4 to 5 minutes, until golden brown and cooked through.

Meanwhile, toast the sesame seeds in a dry skillet for 2 to 3 minutes. Transfer to a pestle and mortar and grind to nearly a paste, but still retaining some texture. Add the sugar, soy sauce, dashi, and citrus juice and grind to incorporate all the flavors.

Place the spiralized daikon and the choy sum and bok choy in a steamer over a pan of boiling water. Steam for 3 to 4 minutes or until tender.

Divide the daikon noodles and greens between 2 plates and drizzle with the dressing. Place the cod on top and serve immediately.

# zucchini spaghetti with prosciutto, asparagus, and peas

**Serves 2**
**Prepare in 5 minutes**
**Cook in 5 to 7 minutes**

2 zucchini, ends trimmed and halved widthwise

½ cup ricotta cheese

2 tablespoons fresh pesto sauce

½ lb asparagus

2 teaspoons olive oil

4 slices prosciutto, chopped

⅔ cup fresh peas

4 basil leaves, torn

salt and freshly ground black pepper

freshly grated Parmesan cheese, to serve

Using a spiralizer fitted with an ⅛-inch spaghetti blade, spiralize the zucchini. Set aside.

In a small bowl, mix together the ricotta and pesto sauce. Set aside.

Snap the woody ends off of the asparagus stalks and discard. Cut off the top 1 ½ inches of each asparagus stalk and set aside. Finely chop the remaining stalks.

Heat the oil in a large skillet or wok, add the chopped asparagus stalks and the prosciutto, and gently fry for 2 to 3 minutes or until the prosciutto is crispy.

Meanwhile, bring a small saucepan of lightly salted water to a boil and add the asparagus tips and peas. Cook for 3 minutes, until tender. Drain well.

Add the zucchini spaghetti to the chopped asparagus and prosciutto and stir-fry for 2 to 3 minutes until just tender. Then add the asparagus tips and peas along with the ricotta and pesto sauce. Stir to coat the vegetables in the sauce.

Divide the zucchini spaghetti between 2 bowls, scatter with the basil, and sprinkle with the Parmesan and pepper. Serve immediately.

*This low-carb paella makes a fantastic recipe for entertaining and can be cooked in no time at all.*

# seafood paella with butternut squash rice

Using a spiralizer fitted with an ⅛-inch spaghetti blade, spiralize the onion and squash, keeping them separate. Place the spiralized squash in a food processor and pulse until it resembles rice.

Place the saffron in a small bowl, add the measurement water, and let soak.

Heat the oil in a large skillet with a lid. Add the chorizo, spiralized onion, and garlic and cook over medium heat for 3 to 4 minutes, until the paprika oil has been released from the chorizo and the onion has softened. Add the squash rice, saffron water, and paprika and cook for 1 minute, then stir in the tomatoes and peas.

Place the cod, shrimp, and squid rings on top of the rice, cover, and cook for 3 minutes. Stir gently, then place the mussels on top, discarding any that are cracked or don't shut when tapped. Cover and cook for 2 to 3 minutes or until all the mussels have opened, the shrimp and fish are cooked through, and the rice is tender. Discard any mussels that remain closed.

Divide the paella between 4 bowls, scatter with the parsley, and serve immediately with lemon wedges for squeezing.

**Serves 4**
**Prepare in 10 minutes**
**Cook in 8 to 12 minutes**

1 onion, ends trimmed

½ butternut squash (the non-bulbous end), about 14½ oz, peeled and halved widthwise

pinch of saffron threads

1 tablespoon hot water

1 tablespoon olive oil

3 oz chorizo, diced

1 garlic clove, crushed

1 teaspoon smoked paprika

1 x 14 oz can diced tomatoes

⅓ cup frozen peas

4 oz boneless, skinless cod fillet, cut into 1-inch pieces

12 raw peeled jumbo shrimp

5 oz squid rings

5 oz mussels, scrubbed and beards removed

2 tablespoons chopped flat-leaf parsley, to garnish

lemon wedges, to serve

# salmon teriyaki with zucchini and sesame noodles

In a shallow nonmetallic dish, mix together all the marinade ingredients, then add the salmon fillets. Turn them over gently to coat thoroughly and let stand to marinate for 15 minutes.

Meanwhile, line a baking pan with nonstick parchment paper. Using a spiralizer fitted with a ¼-inch flat noodle blade, spiralize the zucchini. Set aside.

Place the salmon on the prepared baking pan and drizzle some of the marinade over it. Bake in a preheated oven at 400°F for 5 minutes. Drizzle the remaining marinade over the salmon, return to the oven and cook for a further 5 to 7 minutes, until the salmon is opaque and the fish flakes easily.

Toward the end of the cooking time, heat the sesame oil in a wok or large skillet, add the spiralized zucchini, edamame beans, and sesame seeds and stir-fry for 3 to 4 minutes, until the zucchini noodles are just tender.

Divide the zucchini noodles among 2 plates, place a salmon fillet on top of each, and drizzle with any remaining sauce in the baking pan. Serve immediately.

**Serves 2**

**Prepare in 10 minutes, plus marinating**

**Cook in 10 to 12 minutes**

2 boneless, skinless salmon fillets, about 5 oz each

2 zucchini, ends trimmed and halved widthwise

2 teaspoons sesame oil

1 cup frozen edamame beans

2 teaspoons sesame seeds

### For the marinade

2 tablespoons gluten-free dark soy sauce

1 tablespoon mirin or rice wine vinegar

1 tablespoon honey

1 garlic clove, crushed

2 teaspoons finely grated ginger root

# creamy Marsala mushrooms on parsnip noodles

**Serves 2**

**Prepare in 5 minutes**

**Cook in 13 to 15 minutes**

2 parsnips, peeled, ends trimmed, and halved widthwise

1 teaspoon olive oil

1 tablespoon butter

1 garlic clove, crushed

½ lb mixed mushrooms, such as cremini and portabello, sliced

3 tablespoons Marsala wine or sherry

3 tablespoons reduced-fat crème fraîche

¼ cup water

1 tablespoon chopped tarragon

salt and freshly ground black pepper

Using a spiralizer fitted with a ¼-inch flat noodle blade, spiralize the parsnips.

Heat the oil and butter in a large skillet. When the butter starts to foam, add the garlic and mushrooms and cook over high heat for 5 to 6 minutes, stirring occasionally, until the mushrooms are lightly browned. Stir in the Marsala or sherry, bring to a boil, and simmer for 2 minutes. Add the crème fraîche and stir until blended in.

Stir in the spiralized parsnips and measurement water and cook for a further 5 to 6 minutes, until just tender, stirring occasionally and adding a little more water if the sauce becomes too dry. Stir in the tarragon and season to taste with salt and pepper. Serve immediately.

# Thai green chicken and butternut squash curry

Using a spiralizer fitted with a ¼-inch flat noodle blade, spiralize the butternut squash and zucchini, keeping them separate.

Heat the oil in a saucepan, add the Thai green curry paste, and cook for 1 to 2 minutes, stirring constantly. Stir in the chicken and cook for 2 to 3 minutes, until lightly browned. Add the coconut milk, lemongrass, lime leaves, and fish sauce. Bring to a boil, then reduce the heat and simmer for about 8 minutes, until the sauce has reduced slightly.

Stir in the spiralized squash, cover, and let simmer for 3 minutes, then stir in the spiralized zucchini. Cover and let simmer for a further 2 to 3 minutes, until the vegetables are just tender and the chicken is cooked through. Stir in the basil or cilantro and serve immediately.

**Serves 4**
**Prepare in 5 minutes**
**Cook in 18 to 20 minutes**

½ butternut squash (the non-bulbous end), about 1 lb, peeled and halved widthwise

1 zucchini, ends trimmed and halved widthwise

2 teaspoons peanut or vegetable oil

2 tablespoons gluten-free Thai green curry paste

3 boneless, skinless chicken breasts, cut into thin strips

1 x 14 fl oz can coconut milk

1 lemongrass stalk, tough outer layers removed and coarsely chopped

2 kaffir lime leaves, thinly sliced

2 teaspoons gluten-free fish sauce

handful of Thai basil or cilantro leaves

*The zucchini replaces the pasta in this low-carb meal. If you prefer, you can replace the beef with lean ground turkey.*

# beef, zucchini ribbon, and three-cheese lasagna

**Serves 4**
**Prepare in 15 minutes**
**Cook in 50 to 55 minutes**

4 large zucchini, ends trimmed and
    halved widthwise

1 tablespoon olive oil

1 onion, ends trimmed

1 carrot, peeled, ends trimmed,
    and halved widthwise

1 lb lean ground beef

1 garlic clove, crushed

½ cup red wine

1 x 14 oz can diced tomatoes

2 tablespoons tomato paste

2 teaspoons dried mixed herbs

11 ½ oz ricotta cheese

¾ cup grated Parmesan cheese,
    divided

8 oz mozzarella cheese, sliced

salt and freshly ground black
    pepper

Line 2 large cookie sheets with nonstick parchment paper.

Using a spiralizer fitted with a ribbon blade, spiralize the zucchini and place it in a large bowl. Add the oil and a little salt, and toss to coat the zucchini in the oil and seasoning.

Spread out the zucchini in a single layer on the prepared cookie sheets and bake in a preheated oven at 350°F for 20 minutes, turning the zucchini over and swapping over the cookie sheets in the oven halfway through the cooking time. Remove from the oven and pat the zucchini dry with paper towels. Set aside.

Meanwhile, spiralize the onion and carrot using the ⅛-inch spaghetti blade, keeping them separate.

Place the beef, spiralized onion, and garlic in a large saucepan and dry-fry over medium heat for 3 to 4 minutes, until the beef is browned. Add the spiralized carrot and stir in the wine. Simmer for 2 minutes, then add the tomatoes, tomato paste, and herbs and season with salt and pepper. Bring to a boil, then reduce the heat, cover, and simmer for 15 minutes or until the sauce has reduced and is thick.

In a bowl, beat together the ricotta with ½ cup of the Parmesan.

To assemble the lasagne, place half the beef sauce in the bottom of a 1-quart baking dish, add half the zucchini, cover with the mozzarella, and spread the remaining beef and zucchini on top. Spread the ricotta mixture over the top, then sprinkle with the remaining Parmesan.

Bake in the oven for 30 to 35 minutes, until golden and bubbling. Let stand for 5 minutes before serving.

*Roasting the butternut squash and cauliflower rice helps intensify the flavors and drive off excess water.*

# butternut squash with cauliflower and cheese

**Serves 2**

**Prepare in 10 minutes**

**Cook in 15 minutes**

large chunk of butternut squash (the non-bulbous end), about 10 oz, peeled and halved widthwise

3 oz chorizo, sliced

14½ oz cauliflower florets

½ cup low fat cream cheese

1 cup 2% reduced fat milk

¾ cup grated reduced-fat sharp Cheddar cheese, divided

2 cups baby spinach

4 cherry tomatoes, halved

salt and freshly ground black pepper

mixed salad leaves, to serve

Using a spiralizer fitted with a ¼-inch flat noodle blade, spiralize the squash. Spread out the spiralized squash in a single layer on a nonstick baking pan with the chorizo.

Line a large baking pan with nonstick parchment paper. Place the cauliflower in a food processor and pulse until it resembles rice. Spread out the cauliflower rice on the prepared baking pan.

Place both baking pans in a preheated oven at 400°F for 12 minutes, stirring halfway through, until the cauliflower rice is dried out and starting to crisp and the chorizo is crispy.

Meanwhile, place the cream cheese, milk, and half the Cheddar in a saucepan and season with salt and pepper. Stir over a low heat until the mixture is combined.

Stir the squash noodles, chorizo, cauliflower rice, and spinach into the cheese mixture and stir gently, until the spinach starts to wilt. Transfer to a 1-quart ovenproof dish, scatter with the remaining cheese and top with the tomatoes. Place under a preheated hot broiler and cook for 3 to 4 minutes, until golden and bubbling. Serve immediately with a mixed salad.

# Sicilian anchovy, lemon, parsley, and chile zucchini spaghetti

Using a spiralizer fitted with an ⅛-inch spaghetti blade, spiralize the zucchini.

Drain the olive oil from the anchovies into a large skillet, add the garlic, and cook over medium heat for 1 minute, then add the anchovies. Cook for 2 to 3 minutes, until the anchovies begin to soften and cook down. Stir in the chile flakes, if using, the parsley, and lemon juice.

Add the spiralized zucchini and mix well. Stir in most of the Parmesan, reserving a little. Cook for 2 minutes, until the zucchini spaghetti is al dente, then season to taste with pepper.

Divide the zucchini spaghetti among 2 bowls, sprinkle with the reserved Parmesan, and serve immediately with an arugula salad.

**Serves 2**
**Prepare in 5 minutes**
**Cook in 6 minutes**

2 large zucchini, ends trimmed and halved widthwise

1 x 2 oz can anchovy fillets in olive oil

1 garlic clove, crushed

pinch of dried red chile flakes (optional)

3 tablespoons chopped flat-leaf parsley

juice of 2 small lemons

¼ cup grated Parmesan cheese

freshly ground black pepper

arugula salad, to serve

*This lightly spiced Cajun rice dish is easy to make as it is cooked in one pan. This recipe substitutes carrot rice for long-grain rice.*

# chicken, chorizo, and carrot rice jambalaya

**Serves 4**
**Prepare in 10 minutes**
**Cook in 15 to 18 minutes**

2 large carrots, peeled, ends trimmed, and halved widthwise

1 onion, ends trimmed

1 teaspoon sunflower oil

3½ oz chorizo, chopped

3 boneless, skinless chicken breasts, cut into small cubes

1 tablespoon gluten-free Cajun seasoning

1 red bell pepper, cored, seeded, and diced

1 green pepper, cored, seeded, and diced

1 x 14 oz can diced tomatoes

⅓ cup frozen peas

6 scallions, chopped

3½ oz cooked peeled shrimp

Using a spiralizer fitted with an ⅛-inch spaghetti blade, spiralize the carrots and onion, keeping them separate. Place the spiralized carrots in a food processor. Pulse until the mixture resembles rice.

Heat the oil in a large skillet, add the chorizo and spiralized onion, and cook over medium heat for 3 to 4 minutes, until the onion has softened and the paprika oil has been released from the chorizo. Add the chicken and Cajun spice and cook for 3 to 4 minutes, until the chicken is lightly browned. Stir in the bell peppers and cook for 2 minutes, then add the carrot rice, tomatoes, peas, and scallions, reserving a few scallions. Stir to combine.

Simmer for 5 minutes, stirring occasionally. Stir in the shrimp and cook for 2 minutes, until the vegetables are tender and the chicken is cooked through. Serve scattered with the reserved scallions.

# pork medallions with creamy apple and hard cider sauce

**Serves 2**

**Prepare in 5 minutes**

**Cook in 15 to 18 minutes**

2 parsnips, peeled, ends trimmed, and halved widthwise

1 red eating apple, ends trimmed

1 tablespoon sunflower oil

1 tablespoon butter

8 oz pork fillet, cut into ½-inch thick slices

1 cup medium-dry hard cider or apple juice

2 tablespoons chopped sage

¼ cup crème fraîche

salt and freshly ground black pepper

Using a spiralizer fitted with a ¼-inch flat noodle blade, spiralize the parsnips, keeping them separate. Change to the ribbon blade and spiralize the apple. Coarsely snip any really long ribbons in half using scissors.

Heat the oil and butter in a large skillet with a lid. Add the pork and cook over high heat for 2 to 3 minutes on each side, until browned. Add the spiralized parsnips and cook for 2 to 3 minutes, stirring continuously. Pour in the hard cider or apple juice and add the sage and spiralized apple. Bring to a boil, then reduce the heat to medium, cover, and simmer for 5 to 6 minutes, until the sauce has reduced, the vegetables are tender, and the pork is cooked through.

Stir in the crème fraîche and simmer for 2 minutes, until heated through. Season to taste with salt and pepper and serve immediately.

*Remember to remove the pan from the heat before adding the egg mixture or it will turn into scrambled eggs!*

# spiralized sweet potato carbonara

**Serves 2**
**Prepare in 10 minutes**
**Cook in 10 minutes**

1 large sweet potato, about 14½ oz, peeled, ends trimmed, and halved widthwise

2 eggs

2 tablespoons light cream

½ cup grated Parmesan cheese

1 teaspoon olive oil

4 oz cubed smoked pancetta or chopped bacon

2 garlic cloves, crushed

freshly ground black pepper

1 tablespoon chopped flat-leaf parsley, to garnish

Using a spiralizer fitted with an ⅛-inch spaghetti blade, spiralize the sweet potato.

Place the spiralized sweet potato in a steamer over a pan of simmering water and cook for 5 to 6 minutes or until just tender.

Meanwhile, in a small bowl, beat together the eggs, cream, and Parmesan and season with pepper. Set aside.

Heat the oil in a saucepan, add the pancetta or bacon, and cook for 2 to 3 minutes, until crisp. Stir in the garlic and cook for 1 minute. Add the spiralized sweet potatoes and stir to coat in the bacon and garlic mixture, then remove the pan from the heat.

Gently stir in the egg and cheese mixture to combine. Serve immediately with extra pepper and scattered with parsley.

*I have replaced traditional wheat noodles with low-carb daikon noodles in this hearty Japanese-inspired broth.*

# chile beef daikon ramen

Using a spiralizer fitted with a ¼-inch flat noodle blade, spiralize the daikon. Set aside.

Place the bean sprouts in a sieve and pour boiling water over them, then refresh under cold running water. Set aside to drain.

Place the stock in a large saucepan over high heat. Add the chili sauce, ginger, and garlic, bring to a boil, and then let simmer for 5 minutes.

Meanwhile, brush the steaks with a little oil and season with salt and pepper. Heat a heavy skillet over high heat until smoking hot. Add the steaks and cook for 2 to 3 minutes on each side, until browned but still pink in the middle. (Alternatively, cook for 1 to 2 minutes on each side, if you prefer your steak rare.) Transfer the steaks to a plate, brush them with the teriyaki sauce, and let rest.

Add the mushrooms, bok choy, and spiralized daikon to the chili broth. Let simmer for 5 minutes, until the vegetables are tender.

Slice the steaks thinly. Divide the daikon noodles between 2 bowls and ladle in the broth. Top each serving with the steak strips, bean sprouts, scallions, chile, and cilantro. Serve immediately with the lime wedges for squeezing, on the side.

**Serves 2**
**Prepare in 10 minutes**
**Cook in 10 to 12 minutes**

1 daikon, about ¾ lb, peeled, ends trimmed, and halved widthwise

1 ¼ cups bean sprouts

1 quart hot chicken stock

1 tablespoon hot chili sauce, or to taste

1-inch piece fresh ginger root, peeled and cut into thin matchsticks

1 garlic clove, crushed

2 teaspoons olive oil, for brushing

2 porterhouse or sirloin steaks, about 7 oz each, trimmed of fat

2 tablespoons teriyaki sauce

¼ lb shiitake mushrooms, sliced

7 oz bok choy, sliced

3 scallions, thinly sliced

a few slices red chile

1 small bunch of fresh cilantro

salt and freshly ground black pepper

2 lime wedges, to serve

*Spiralizing the squash and making it into rice transforms this usually carb-heavy dish into a lighter alternative.*

# butternut squash and spinach rice-free risotto

(gf) (lc) (v)

**Serves 2**
**Prepare in 10 minutes**
**Cook in 10 to 12 minutes**

1 small onion, ends trimmed

large chunk of butternut squash (the non-bulbous end), about ¾ lb, peeled and halved widthwise

1 tablespoon olive oil

1 garlic clove, crushed

½ cup dry white wine

1 tablespoon chopped sage

1 cup hot gluten-free vegetable stock, divided

5 oz baby spinach

¼ cup grated vegetarian pasta cheese or Parmesan cheese, plus extra to serve

3 oz goat cheese, chopped

salt and freshly ground black pepper

**To serve**
6 crispy fried sage leaves
¼ cup pine nuts, toasted

Using a spiralizer fitted with an ⅛-inch spaghetti blade, spiralize the onion and squash, keeping them separate. This quantity should yield about 11 ½ oz spiralized squash. Place the spiralized squash in a food processor and pulse until it resembles rice.

Heat the oil in a large skillet, add the spiralized onion and garlic, and cook over medium heat for 2 to 3 minutes, until softened. Add the wine and reduce the liquid by half, then add the squash rice and cook for 2 minutes. Add the chopped sage and half the stock and cook until most of the stock has evaporated. Add the remaining stock, season with salt and pepper, and cook for a further 2 to 3 minutes, until the squash is just tender, adding a little more hot water if needed. Add the spinach and vegetarian pasta cheese or Parmesan and stir for about 2 minutes until the spinach has wilted. Stir in the goat cheese and let melt.

Divide the risotto between 2 plates and serve topped with crispy sage leaves, toasted pine nuts, and a sprinkling of extra vegetarian pasta cheese or Parmesan.

# baking and sweet treats

*This cornbread is flecked with chile and scallions.*
*It is very easy to make and contains no yeast.*

# butternut squash and chile cornbread

(v)

**Makes 6 to 8 wedges**
**Prepare in 10 minutes**
**Cook in 25 to 30 minutes**

2 tablespoons coconut oil or melted butter, plus extra for greasing

large chunk of butternut squash (the non-bulbous end), about ½ lb, peeled and halved widthwise

1 cup all-purpose flour

1 cup polenta (cornmeal)

2 teaspoons baking powder

1 teaspoon salt

4 scallions, thinly sliced

1 red chile, seeded and finely chopped

2 eggs

1 cup buttermilk

Grease an 8-inch springform cake pan and line the bottom with nonstick parchment paper.

Using a spiralizer fitted with an ⅛-inch spaghetti blade, spiralize the squash. Coarsely snip any really long spirals in half with scissors.

In a large bowl, mix together the flour, polenta, baking powder, salt, scallions, chile, and spiralized squash.

In a pitcher, beat together the eggs, buttermilk, and oil or melted butter. Add the wet mixture to the dry ingredients and stir well to combine.

Pour the batter into the prepared pan and bake in a preheated oven at 400°F for 25 to 30 minutes, until golden brown, firm, and beginning to pull away from the inside of the pan. Remove from the oven and let cool slightly in the pan.

Serve the cornbread warm, either sliced or cut into wedges.

# sweet banana, butternut squash, and pecan loaf

(v)

**Serves 8 to 10**
**Prepare in 10 minutes**
**Cook in 50 to 60 minutes**

1 stick butter, softened, plus extra
for greasing

large chunk of butternut squash
(the non-bulbous end),
about ½ lb, peeled and
halved widthwise

1 cup soft light brown sugar

2 eggs, lightly beaten

3 ripe bananas, mashed

1 teaspoon vanilla extract

1 cup all-purpose flour

1 cup wholemeal flour

1 teaspoon baking soda

1 teaspoon baking powder

½ teaspoon salt

½ cup pecans, coarsely chopped,
plus 8 whole pecans, to decorate

Grease a 2-pound (9 x 5 inch) loaf pan.

Using a spiralizer fitted with an ⅛-inch spaghetti blade, spiralize the squash. Coarsely snip any really long spirals in half with scissors.

In a large bowl, cream together the butter and sugar until light and fluffy. Gradually beat in the eggs, bananas, and vanilla extract until well combined. Sift in the flours, baking soda, baking powder, and salt and gently fold in. Stir in the chopped pecans and spiralized squash.

Spoon the batter into the prepared pan and arrange the pecan halves in a line down the center. Bake in a preheated oven at 350°F for 50 to 60 minutes or until risen, golden brown, and a skewer inserted in the center comes out clean. Cover the top with foil if the loaf becomes too brown during cooking.

Let the loaf cool in the pan for a few minutes, then remove from the pan and transfer to a cooling rack to cool completely before serving.

# apple, blackberry, and cinnamon streusel muffins

Line a muffin pan with 10 paper muffin cups.

To make the streusel topping, place the flour in a small bowl, add the butter, and rub it in with your fingertips until the mixture resembles fine bread crumbs. Stir in the sugar and set aside.

Using a spiralizer fitted with a ¼-inch flat noodle blade, spiralize the apples.

In a large bowl, sift together the flour, baking powder, and salt. Then stir in the cinnamon and sugar. In a large measuring cup, beat together the egg, milk, and oil and then add the mixture to the dry ingredients. Stir until just combined and then stir in the spiralized apples and the blackberries. Divide the batter among the muffin cups and sprinkle the top of each with the streusel topping. Bake the muffins in a preheated oven at 375°F for 20 to 25 minutes until risen and firm.

(V)

**Makes 10**
**Prepare in 10 minutes**
**Cook in 20 to 25 minutes**

2 red eating apples, ends trimmed

2½ cups all-purpose flour

1 tablespoon baking powder

½ teaspoon salt

1 teaspoon ground cinnamon

½ cup superfine sugar

1 large egg

1 cup milk

⅓ cup sunflower oil

1 cup blackberries

**For the streusel topping**

3½ tablespoons all-purpose flour

1 tablespoon cold butter

2 tablespoons light brown sugar

# zucchini and Cheddar cheese soda bread

(v)

**Makes 1 medium loaf**
**Prepare in 10 minutes**
**Cook in 25 to 30 minutes**

1 large zucchini, ends trimmed and halved widthwise

2 cups wholemeal flour

2 cups all-purpose flour, plus extra for dusting

½ teaspoon sea salt

1 teaspoon superfine sugar

1 teaspoon baking soda

¾ cup grated sharp Cheddar cheese, divided

1 ¾ cups buttermilk, plus extra for brushing

Using a spiralizer fitted with an ⅛-inch spaghetti blade, spiralize the zucchini. Place the spiralized zucchini on a clean dish cloth or paper towels and gently squeeze out any excess liquid.

Place a large casserole dish and its lid in a preheated oven at 425°F.

In a large bowl, mix together the spiralized zucchini, flours, salt, sugar, baking soda and ½ cup of the cheese using your hands. Stir in enough of the buttermilk to bring the mixture together to make a soft dough.

Tip the dough out onto a lightly floured surface and knead lightly, then shape into a shallow round loaf about 1 ½ inches thick. Make a cross in the top, brush with a little buttermilk, and sprinkle with the remaining cheese.

Wearing oven mitts, carefully remove the hot casserole dish from the oven and dust the inside lightly with flour. Gently lower the dough into the dish, cover with the heated lid, and return to the oven. Bake for about 25 to 30 minutes, until the loaf is golden and sounds hollow when tapped.

Let cool in the dish for 5 minutes, then transfer the bread to a cooling rack to cool slightly. This bread is best served warm.

*The beet rice makes these cupcakes a pretty color. They are best eaten on the day they are made.*

# beet and vanilla cupcakes

**Makes 18**

**Prepare in 15 minutes, plus cooling**

**Cook in 18 to 20 minutes**

2 fresh beets, scrubbed and ends trimmed

1½ sticks unsalted butter, softened

¾ cup superfine sugar

2 large eggs, beaten

1 tablespoon vanilla extract

1½ cups all-purpose flour sifted with 1½ teaspoons baking powder

**For the frosting**

¾ cup reduced-fat cream cheese

2 tablespoons confectioners' sugar, sifted

1 tablespoon vanilla extract

Line 1 or 2 cupcake pans with 18 paper baking cups.

Using a spiralizer fitted with an ⅛-inch spaghetti blade, spiralize the beets. Reserve a few spirals for decoration and add the remainder to a food processor. Pulse them until they resemble rice.

In a large bowl, beat together the butter and sugar until light and fluffy. Beat in the eggs, a little at a time, then beat in the vanilla extract. Sift in the flour and stir until just combined, then fold in the beet rice.

Divide the mixture among the baking cups. Bake in a preheated oven at 350°F for 18 to 20 minutes, until risen and golden brown. Remove from the oven and transfer to a wire rack to cool completely.

To make the frosting, place all the frosting ingredients in a bowl and beat together until smooth. Spread the frosting over the cooled cupcakes and decorate with the reserved beet spirals.

*The addition of spiralized carrots to this gluten-free cake makes it deliciously moist.*

# orange, carrot, and almond cake

**Serves 8 to 10**

**Prepare in 20 minutes, plus cooling**

**Cook in about 2½ hours**

2 oranges

butter, for greasing

2 carrots, peeled, ends trimmed, and halved widthwise

4 eggs

1½ cups superfine sugar

3 cups ground almonds

1 teaspoon gluten-free baking powder

4 cardamom pods, seeds crushed

**For the syrup**

grated zest and juice of 1 orange

3½ cups superfine sugar

2 tablespoons water

1 teaspoon orange blossom water

Place the oranges in a large saucepan over medium heat and add boiling water to cover. Cover the pan with a lid and let the oranges simmer for 1 hour or until tender. Drain and let cool.

Grease an 8-inch springform cake pan and line the bottom with nonstick parchment paper. Using a spiralizer fitted with an ⅛-inch spaghetti blade, spiralize the carrots. Coarsely snip any really long spirals in half using scissors.

Cut the cooled oranges in half and remove any seeds. Place in a food processor and purée until smooth.

In a large mixing bowl, beat together the eggs and sugar with an electric hand mixer until thick and pale. Gently fold in the puréed oranges, the spiralized carrots (reserving a few spirals for decoration), the ground almonds, baking powder, and cardamom until combined.

Spoon the batter into the prepared pan and bake in the center of a preheated oven at 325°F for about 1 to 1¼ hours or until a skewer inserted in the center comes out clean. Cover the top with foil if it becomes too brown during baking. Remove from the oven and let the cake cool completely in the pan.

To make the syrup, place the orange juice, sugar, and measurement water in a saucepan. Cook over low heat, stirring, for 5 minutes or until the sugar has dissolved and the syrup thickened slightly. Remove from the heat, stir in the orange blossom water, orange zest, and reserved carrot spirals and let stand to cool.

Remove the cake from the pan and drizzle it with the syrup.

*These tasty cookies are made with very little added sugar and are lower in fat than traditional cookies.*

# sweet potato and chocolate chip cookies

Line 2 large cookie sheets with nonstick parchment paper.

Using a spiralizer fitted with an ⅛-inch spaghetti blade, spiralize the sweet potato. Place the spiralized sweet potato in a food processor and pulse until it resembles rice.

Add the sweet potato rice to a bowl along with the oats, cinnamon or mixed spice, and chocolate chips. Stir to combine.

In a small bowl, beat together the eggs, almond butter, honey, and vanilla extract. Add to the sweet potato mixture and stir together.

Drop heaped tablespoonfuls of the mixture onto the prepared cookie sheets and flatten slightly. Bake in a preheated oven at 350°F for 10 to 12 minutes, until lightly golden.

Remove from the oven, let the cookies cool on the sheets for 5 minutes, and then transfer to a wire rack to cool completely. The cookies will keep for up to 2 days in an airtight container.

**Makes about 15**
**Prepare in 10 minutes**
**Cook in 10 to 12 minutes**

1 sweet potato, about ½ lb, peeled, ends trimmed, and halved widthwise

⅓ cup gluten-free rolled oats

½ teaspoon ground cinnamon or mixed spice

½ cup gluten-free dark chocolate chips

2 eggs, beaten

3 tablespoons almond butter

1 tablespoon honey

1 teaspoon vanilla extract

*The addition of an earthy beet to these brownie-inspired cookies really intensifies the chocolate flavor.*

# crackled beet brownie cookies

**Makes 12 to 14**

**Prepare in 10 minutes, plus freezing**

**Cook in 10 to 12 minutes**

1 fresh beet, scrubbed and ends trimmed

½ cup unsweetened cocoa powder

1⅓ packed cups soft light brown sugar

¼ cup coconut or sunflower oil

2 eggs

1 teaspoon vanilla extract

1 cup all-purpose flour

1 teaspoon baking powder

¼ cup confectioners' sugar

Using a spiralizer fitted with an ⅛-inch spaghetti blade, spiralize the beet. Coarsely snip any really long spirals with scissors and place in a large freezerproof bowl.

Place all the remaining ingredients, except the confectioners' sugar, in a food processor and pulse until well combined. Stir the mixture into the spiralized beet and freeze for about 30 minutes. Alternatively, you can chill the mixture in the refrigerator for about 2 hours.

Line 2 large cookie sheets with nonstick parchment paper. Remove the mixture from the freezer and roll into golfball-sized balls. Sift the confectioners' sugar onto a plate, then roll each ball in the confectioners' sugar.

Place the balls, spaced well apart, on the prepared cookie sheets and flatten slightly using a fork. Bake in a preheated oven at 350°F for 10 to 12 minutes, until set.

Remove from the oven and let the cookies cool on the cookie sheets for a few minutes, then transfer to a wire rack to cool completely. The cookies will keep for up to 2 to 3 days in an airtight container.

*This dessert is so simple to make yet looks spectacular.*
*Prepare just before serving to stop the apples from browning.*

# apple carpaccio with lime and mint sugar

Using a spiralizer fitted with a ribbon blade, spiralize the apples. Arrange across a large platter and sprinkle with freshly squeezed lime juice.

Place the sugar, lime zest, and mint in a food processor and blend to make a bright green sugar. Sprinkle the apples with the mint sugar and serve immediately.

(gf) (v) (vg)

**Serves 4 to 6**

**Prepare in 10 minutes**

4 red or pink eating apples, ends
   trimmed

grated zest and juice of 1 lime

2 tablespoons superfine sugar

2 heaped tablespoons mint leaves

*These lovely little puddings are deliciously sticky and moist. Perfect for entertaining.*

# carrot and ginger steamed puddings

Using a spiralizer fitted with an ⅛-inch spaghetti blade, spiralize the carrot. This should yield about 5 ounces of spiralized carrot. Coarsely snip any long spirals into shorter lengths with scissors.

Grease 4 x 5-ounce metal pudding bowls, then add 1 tablespoon ginger syrup to the bottom of each.

In a large bowl, beat together the butter and sugar until light and fluffy. Gradually beat in the eggs. Gently fold in the flour, milk, stem ginger, and spiralized carrot.

Divide the mixture among the prepared pudding bowls, then cover each tightly with foil and place in a roasting pan. Pour enough boiling water into the pan to rise ¾ inch up the side of the bowls. Bake in a preheated oven at 350°F for 30 to 35 minutes or until a skewer inserted in the center comes out clean.

Let the puddings cool in the pans for 5 minutes, then run a knife around the inside of the pans to loosen them. Invert the puddings out onto serving plates and drizzle them with extra ginger syrup. Serve immediately with custard or cream.

(v)

**Serves 4**
**Prepare in 10 minutes**
**Cook in 30 to 35 minutes**

1 large carrot, peeled, ends trimmed, and halved widthwise

1 stick butter, softened, plus extra for greasing

¼ cup syrup from a jar of stem ginger in syrup, divided, plus extra to serve

½ cup superfine sugar

2 eggs, beaten

1 cup all-purpose flour sifted with 1 teaspoon baking powder

2 tablespoons milk

4 pieces stem ginger in syrup, drained and finely chopped

custard or cream, to serve

*These fluffy waffles could also be served for breakfast with just a drizzle of maple syrup or honey.*

# apple and blueberry waffles with ice cream

**Serves 2**

**Prepare in 5 minutes**

**Cook in 5 to 6 minutes**

1 red or green eating apple, ends trimmed

2 tablespoons all-purpose flour

1 teaspoon superfine sugar

1 egg, lightly beaten

½ teaspoon vanilla extract

⅓ cup blueberries

a little cooking spray oil or melted butter, for cooking

vanilla ice cream, to serve

Using a spiralizer fitted with a ¼-inch flat noodle blade, spiralize the apple.

Place the flour and sugar in a bowl and gradually stir in the egg and vanilla extract to make a smooth batter. Add the spiralized apples and the blueberries and mix gently until combined.

Preheat a waffle machine following the manufacturer's directions and spray with oil or brush with a little butter. Divide the batter between the 2 waffle plates, being careful not to overfill them, then cook for 5 to 6 minutes, until golden and cooked through.

Serve immediately with scoops of vanilla ice cream.

*For a grown-up frozen treat, add 1 teaspoon of gin or Pimm's to each mold.*

# cucumber, lemon, and mint ice pops

Place the measurement water, lemon juice, and sugar in a saucepan. Cook over low heat, stirring until the sugar has dissolved. Pour into a pitcher and let cool, then stir in the chopped mint.

Using a spiralizer fitted with an ⅛-inch spaghetti blade, spiralize the cucumber.

Divide the spiralized cucumber between 8 ice pop molds, then pour in the lemon and mint mixture to come nearly to the top of each mold. Add a wooden stick to each and place in the freezer for 3 to 4 hours or until frozen.

**Makes 8**

**Prepare in 10 minutes, plus cooling and freezing**

**Cook in 5 minutes**

1 ¾ cups water

juice of 2 large lemons

¼ cup superfine sugar

10 mint leaves, finely chopped

½ cucumber, ends trimmed and halved widthwise

# green plantain rice pudding with coconut and mango

**Serves 2 to 3**
**Prepare in 5 minutes**
**Cook in 15 minutes**

2 green plantains (the straightest ones you can find)

1 x 14 fl oz can coconut milk

1 cup water

6 green cardamom pods, crushed

2 tablespoons superfine sugar

**To serve**
toasted coconut shavings
fresh chopped mango

Cut the plantains in half widthwise. Score the outside of the skin and peel off, then trim the ends. Using a spiralizer fitted with an 1/8-inch spaghetti blade, spiralize the plantains. Place the spiralized plantains in a food processor and pulse until the mixture resembles rice.

Pour the coconut milk into a pitcher, stir well, and then add the measurement water to make up to 2½ cups.

Place the plantain rice in a saucepan, then stir in 1¾ cups of the coconut milk mixture, the cardamoms, and sugar. Bring to a boil, then reduce the heat to low and simmer for 10 minutes, stirring occasionally and adding a little more of the coconut milk if the mixture starts sticking to the bottom of the pan. Add the remaining coconut milk and simmer for a further 2 minutes, until the mixture is creamy and the plantain rice is cooked.

Serve the rice pudding topped with coconut shavings and fresh chopped mango.

# dark chocolate and pear dessert with crisp topping and ice cream

First, make the crisp topping. Place the flour in a bowl, add the butter, and rub it in with your fingertips until the mixture resembles fine bread crumbs. Stir in the remaining crisp ingredients and set aside.

Grease 6 x 8-ounce ovenproof teacups or ramekins. Using a spiralizer fitted with a ¼-inch flat noodle blade, spiralize the pears.

Place the spiralized pears in a bowl and mix together with the lemon zest and juice, sugar, and chocolate. Divide the pear mixture among the prepared teacups or ramekins, drizzling them with any remaining juice.

Spoon the crisp topping onto the pears and press down lightly. Place the crisps on a cookie sheet and bake in a preheated oven at 350°F for 15 minutes, until golden and bubbling. Serve with a scoop of vanilla ice cream.

(V)

**Serves 6**
**Prepare in 15 minutes**
**Cook in 15 minutes**

4 firm pears, pointed ends trimmed

grated zest and juice of 1 lemon

⅓ cup soft light brown sugar

⅓ cup dark chocolate chips or 2 oz chocolate chunks

vanilla ice cream, to serve

**For the crisp topping**

½ cup all-purpose flour

½ stick cold butter, diced, plus extra for greasing

⅓ cup rolled oats

⅓ cup soft light brown sugar

⅓ cup dark chocolate chips or 2 oz chocolate chunks

½ cup roasted hazelnuts, chopped

*This tart is so easy to make and looks really impressive. Serve with vanilla ice cream.*

# spiralized apple puff pastry tart

**Serves 6 to 8**

**Prepare in 10 minutes**

**Cook in 15 to 20 minutes**

1 x 10½-oz package ready-rolled puff pastry

2 red or green eating apples, ends trimmed

juice of 1 lemon

½ stick butter, diced

3 tablespoons superfine sugar

¼ cup apricot jam

vanilla ice cream, to serve

Unroll the pastry and place on a nonstick cookie sheet. Using a sharp knife, score a 1-inch border around the edges, being careful not to cut all the way through.

Using a spiralizer fitted with a ribbon blade, spiralize the apples and place them in a bowl. Sprinkle with the lemon juice and toss gently to coat.

Dot some of the butter over the pastry and sprinkle with 1 tablespoon of the sugar. Arrange the apples on the pastry, then dot them with the remaining butter, and sprinkle evenly with the remaining sugar.

Bake in a preheated oven at 425°F for 15 to 20 minutes until the pastry is risen, golden, and crisp.

Warm the apricot jam in a small saucepan, then brush it evenly over the apples and pastry. Serve immediately with scoops of vanilla ice cream.

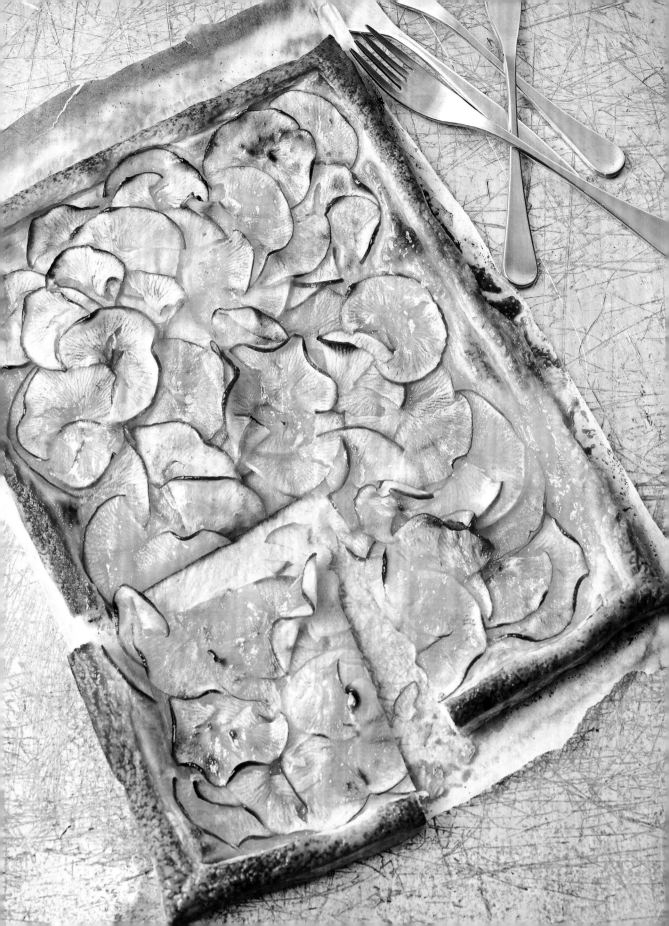

*This delicious marmalade is perfect for spreading on toast.*
*It will keep for up to 2 years sealed in a jar.*

# butternut squash and orange marmalade

If using pumpkin, cut it into large chunks. Using a spiralizer fitted with an ⅛-inch spaghetti blade, spiralize the squash or pumpkin. This should yield about 1 ½ pounds spiralized squash or pumpkin.

Place the spiralized squash or pumpkin in a preserving pan or wide saucepan. Add the oranges, lemon juice, ginger, if using, and the measurement water. Bring to a boil, then reduce the heat and let simmer for 20 to 25 minutes, or until the oranges are tender.

Add the sugar and cook over low heat, stirring until it has dissolved. Increase the heat to high and bring to a boil, then reduce the heat to medium and simmer for 25 to 30 minutes or until the mixture is thick and syrupy and leaves a clear channel when a wooden spoon is drawn through it.

Let the marmalade cool in the pan for 5 minutes, then carefully ladle into hot sterilized jars and seal.

**Makes about 4 x 8-ounce jars**
**Prepare in 15 minutes**
**Cook in about 1 hour**

1 large or 2 medium butternut squash (the non-bulbous end) or pumpkin, peeled and halved widthwise

2 oranges, thinly sliced and halved

juice of 2 lemons

3 oz fresh root ginger, peeled and thinly sliced (optional)

2½ cups water

3½ cups granulated sugar

*This instant jam is so quick to make and can be eaten once cooled. Delicious spread on scones or crumpets.*

# quick apple and ginger jam

**Serves 4**

**Prepare in 5 minutes**

**Cook in 10 to 15 minutes**

2 tart cooking apples, peeled and
   ends trimmed

¼ cup superfine sugar, or to taste

2-inch piece fresh ginger root,
   peeled and grated

1 tablespoon lemon juice

Using a spiralizer fitted with a ¼-inch flat noodle blade, spiralize the apples.

Place the spiralized apples in a saucepan with the sugar and ginger. Cook over medium heat, stirring gently, until the sugar has dissolved. Bring to a boil, then reduce the heat and let simmer for 8 to 10 minutes, until the apple is tender.

Stir in the lemon juice and cook for a further 2 to 3 minutes, until the jam has thickened and reduced. Let cool before serving. The jam will keep for up to 2 to 3 days in the refrigerator.

*This cross between a jam and a marmalade is a great way of using up a glut of zucchini.*

# zucchini, lemon, and ginger jam

Using a spiralizer fitted with an ⅛-inch spaghetti blade, spiralize the zucchini. Coarsely snip any really long strands in half with scissors.

Place the spiralized zucchini in a large, deep saucepan or preserving pan along with the ginger and lemon zest and juice. Cook over low heat, stirring occasionally, for 3 to 4 minutes or until the zucchini start to release their liquid.

Add the sugar and cook gently, stirring until it has dissolved. Increase the heat to high and bring to a boil. Let the mixture boil for about 15 to 20 minutes or until the jam has reduced and is glossy. To test whether the jam has set, place a little on a cold saucer and let stand for a few minutes. Gently push the jam with your finger—if it wrinkles, the jam has reached setting point.

Remove from the heat and scoop any foam off of the surface. Let the jam cool in the pan for 10 minutes, then carefully pour it into hot sterilized jars and seal. This jam will keep for up to 1 year.

**Makes about 4 x 14½-ounce jars**

**Prepare in 5 minutes**

**Cook in 20 to 25 minutes**

2¼ lb zucchini, ends trimmed and halved widthwise

3 oz piece fresh ginger root, peeled and grated

finely grated zest and juice of 2 lemons

2¼ lb jelly sugar (sugar with pectin)

# index

# acknowledgments

Thank you to dexam.co.uk for loaning us the spiralizers for the photoshoot.

Editorial Director: Eleanor Maxfield
Project Editor: Clare Churly
Copy Editor: Jo Murray
Art Director: Tracy Killick at Tracy Killick Art Direction and Design
Photographer: William Shaw
Home Economist: Denise Smart
Prop Stylist: Liz Hippisley
Production Manager: Caroline Alberti